Misspent Youth...

1 **Tackling Offending Behaviour**

2 **Preventing Youth Crime**

3 **Developing a Strategy**

Contents

Preface   3

Introduction   5
  Crime and youth crime   5
  Offending by young people   8
  Who is at risk?   8
  Trends in youth crime   11
  Dealing with antisocial
  behaviour by young people   13

1. Tackling Offending Behaviour   15
  Introduction   16
  The criminal justice system
  for young people   17
  Pre-court procedures   19
  – Arrest and interview   19
  – Deciding what to do with the
     young person   20
  – Action by the police   20
  – Prosecution   24
  – Transfers to local authority
     accommodation   24
  – Cases withdrawn,
     discontinued and dismissed   25
  The youth court process   26
  – Youth justice and
     probation services   27
  – Adjournments   29
  – Bail and remand decisions   30
  – Pleas   33
  – Trials   33
  – Pre-sentence reports   34
  – Speeding up the process   35
  Sentences of the court   35
  – Reducing re-offending   35
  – Fines, compensation orders
     and binding over   37
  – Attendance centre orders   38
  – Supervision orders   38
  – Other community sentences   41
  – Custody   42
  Efficiency and effectiveness   42

The criminal justice system
and race   44
A more efficient and effective
approach   46
  – Experience and views of
     young offenders   50
Conclusions   53
Recommendations   54

2. Preventing Youth Crime   57
  Introduction   58
  Family factors   60
  – Improving parenting   62
  Early childhood behaviour   64
  – Structured nursery education
     with home support   65
  Problems at school   66
  – School support   68
  – Reducing truancy and
     exclusion   70
  – The education of 'looked after'
     children   74
  Friends and leisure time   75
  – Youth work   76
  Housing   79
  – Young people leaving care   80
  Training and employment   82
  – Training courses   83
  Drugs and alcohol   85
  – Help with drug and alcohol
     problems   87
  – Reinforcing community
     institutions   88
  Conclusions   89
  Recommendations   91

3. Developing a Strategy   95
  Why a strategy is needed   96
  Co-ordinating programmes to
  prevent youth crime and other
  antisocial behaviour   98
  Sharing information   99

Practical solutions   100
  – Focus on deprived areas   100
  – Strategic co-ordination   101
  – Bottom-up co-ordination   101
  – Strategy for young people   102
  – Funding   102
Conclusions   103
Recommendations   104

Appendix 1:
Research on what works to
reduce re-offending   106
  – References   111

Appendix 2:
Members of the Advisory
Panel   112

References   113

Index   121

© Audit Commission 1996
First published in November 1996 by the
Audit Commission for Local Authorities and the
National Health Service in England and Wales,
1 Vincent Square, London SW1P 2PN

Typeset by Dominic Shearn, IDP, Bath.
Printed in the UK for the Audit
Commission by Bourne Press, Bournemouth.
ISBN 1 86240 007 5

Photographs:
Barbara Laws/John Birdsall
Photography (cover); John Birdsall
Photography (p57, p85); modelled
for the Children's Society (p17, p53);
Format Partners (p77, p80);
Sally & Richard Greenhill (p69);
David Hoffman (p15); Tony Stone
Images (p64, p65, p85, p95).

Preface

'Over the last 18 months, the Commission has been reviewing the implications of the arrangements for young offenders provided by public services, and its findings are set out in this report.'

The Audit Commission oversees the external audit of local authorities, probation services, police forces (except the Metropolitan Police Force) and National Health Service (NHS) agencies in England and Wales. As part of this function, the Commission is required to undertake studies to enable it to make recommendations for improving the economy, efficiency and effectiveness of services provided by these bodies; and it is required to comment on the effects of statutory provisions or guidance by central government on the economy, efficiency and effectiveness of these agencies.

Over the last 18 months, the Commission has been reviewing the implications of the arrangements for young offenders provided by public services, and its findings are set out in this report. It covers the current arrangements for dealing with young offenders, including some agencies – such as the courts – which are not audited by the Commission, as it was considered important to review the system in its entirety.

The study of young people and crime follows previous reviews of services for young people in education, health, social services, police and probation (Exhibit 1, overleaf). Future studies are likely to include the planning of school places and a review of community safety strategies across a range of agencies.

The study on which this report is based was carried out by Mark Perfect and Judy Renshaw of the local government and health studies directorates of the Commission, under the direction of a joint steering group: David Browning, Doug Edmunds, Jonathan Boyce, Peter Wilkinson, Kate Flannery and Steve Evans. Clare Weiss assisted with the study and developed the local audit work. Stuart Bailey and Amanda Hale carried out most of the data analysis. The study team was advised by a group of experts, listed at Appendix 2.

Exhibit 1
Audit Commission reports on services for young people and offenders

The study of young people and crime follows previous reviews of services for young people in education, health, social services, police and probation.

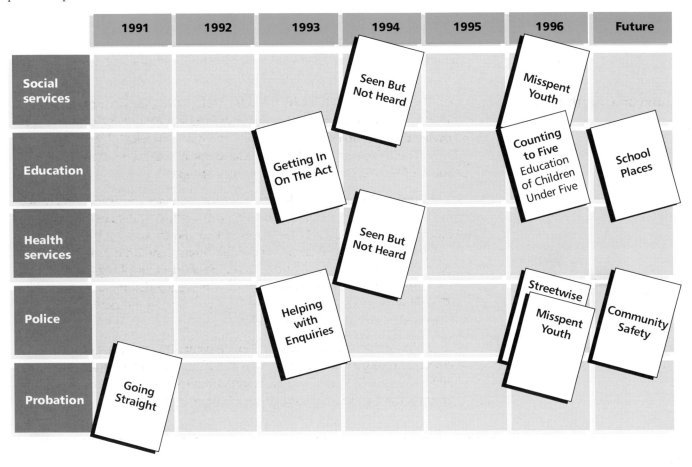

Source: Audit Commission

Introduction

Crimes against individuals have increased and are concentrated in a few areas. A disproportionate number are committed by young people of 10-17 years, especially by a small number of persistent offenders. A variety of central and local agencies are responsible for identifying and dealing with young offenders. They spend around £1 billion a year in response to offending by young people – largely to identify the culprits.

Crime and youth crime

1. Crime is high on the public agenda. One in five adults questioned in the 1996 British Crime Survey was very worried about being burgled, mugged or having their car stolen or broken into. These fears ranked as high as potential job loss and higher than debt and home accidents (Ref.1). So reducing crime, and the fear of crime, is important to many people.

2. Crimes against individuals – such as theft, burglary and assault – increased by 73 per cent between 1981 and 1995 to 19 million in England and Wales, according to the British Crime Survey of households (Exhibit 2). A comparable survey of retailers and manufacturers, conducted in 1993, estimated that they suffer a further 9 million offences, involving losses of over £1 billion (Refs. 5, 6). Together, these surveys suggest that there are more than 28 million offences a year. The costs to public services and victims are estimated to exceed £16 billion (Ref. 7).

3. A disproportionate amount of crime is committed by young people, especially young males. In 1994, two out of every five known offenders were under the age of 21, and a quarter were under 18 (Ref. 8). Assuming the latter group is responsible for a comparable proportion of all offences, offenders

---

Exhibit 2
Crimes against individuals

Crimes against individuals increased by 73 per cent between 1981 and 1995.

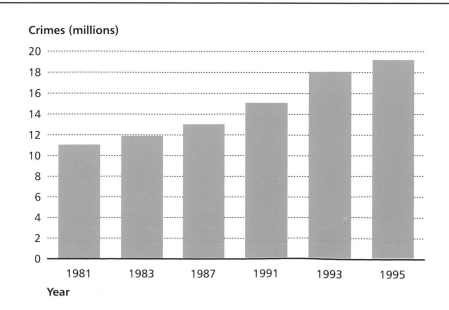

Crimes (millions)

Year

Source: British Crime Survey (Refs. 2, 3, 4)

'Measures to prevent or reduce offending would also help tackle nuisance caused by young people...'

under the age of 18 commit about seven million offences a year against individuals, retailers and manufacturers. They are dealt with separately from adults, by the youth courts, and are the subject of this report.

4. Public services undertake three activities in relation to offending by young people. First, they identify young offenders and go through the process of deciding whether they are guilty and, if so, what to do with them; second, they deal with those who admit their guilt or who are found guilty; and third, they attempt to prevent or reduce offending by young people (Exhibit 3). Measures to prevent or reduce offending would also help tackle nuisance caused by young people. This report examines the distribution of resources between these activities, as well as how efficiently and effectively they are carried out.

5. The responsibility for identifying, and dealing with, young offenders falls across a variety of central and local agencies: police, youth justice services, probation, legal aid, the Crown Prosecution Service (CPS), youth court, crown court and the prison service. These public services spend around £1 billion a year on dealing with offending by young people; around £660 million of this is spent by the police, largely on identifying them (Exhibit 4). The objectives of the different agencies include *punishing* offenders in a manner appropriate to their crimes, according to the 'just deserts' principle of the 1991 Criminal Justice Act – partly to deter others from offending – and *preventing* further offending by young people.

6. Differences in emphasis between the agencies can give rise to tensions. For example, one case observed in the youth court involved the prosecution of a 15-year-old boy who admitted to many small thefts from supermarkets. The thefts took place over a short period following the breakup of the boy's family

Exhibit 3
The responsibilities of public services in relation to youth offending

Public services process young people to decide whether they are guilty and, if so, what to do with them; deal with those who admit their guilt or who are found guilty; and attempt to prevent or reduce offending.

Processing
by police and courts through to a decision

Dealing with those who admit guilt or are found guilty

Preventing offending by young people

Source: Audit Commission

Exhibit 4
Public spending on the criminal justice system for young people

Public services spend around £1 billion a year processing and dealing with offending by young people.

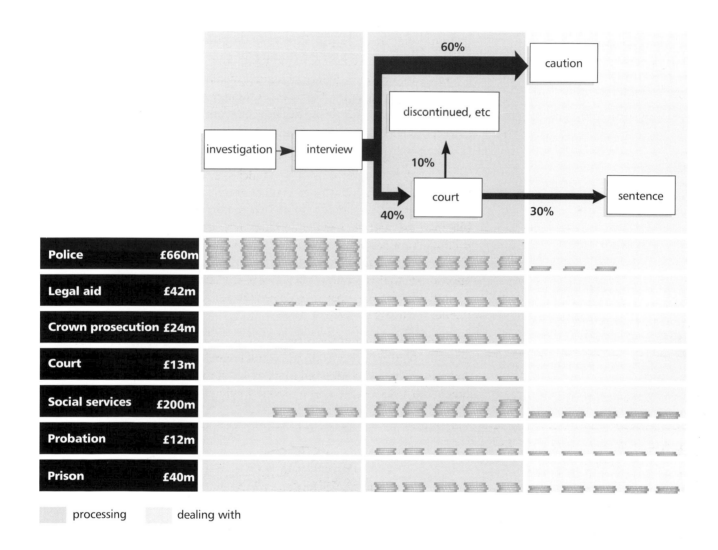

Police £660m

Legal aid £42m

Crown prosecution £24m

Court £13m

Social services £200m

Probation £12m

Prison £40m

processing   dealing with

Source: *Audit Commission estimates, from criminal statistics; annual reports from Home Office; Lord Chancellor's Department; CIPFA*

when he was living with his alcoholic father who kept no food in the house. Before the trial, social services arranged for the boy to live with foster parents. The youth court process put extra pressure on the new foster parents and took up the time of many expensive professionals, without punishing or helping anyone. The objective of following the due process of the criminal law conflicted with the objective of dealing effectively and efficiently with the boy. If the response to young offenders is to be effective, a consistent approach by all of these services is required.

Offending by young people

7. While offending once or twice is common – about half of young men admit to having done so (Ref. 9) – a few persistent offenders commit most of the crimes by young people (Exhibit 5). Five per cent of the young men interviewed by Home Office researchers, who admitted to 20 or more crimes in the previous 12 months, were responsible for at least two-thirds of the offences reported by the whole group (assuming they averaged 25 offences each). However, identifying the most prolific group is difficult, as few young people offend very frequently for more than short periods (Ref. 10).

8. Most offences by young people are property-related (Exhibit 6). Those who persistently engage in offences such as taking cars are not disproportionately engaged in the most serious and violent crimes (Ref. 11). Only a few young offenders commit the most serious types of crime: in January 1996, only four were being held in secure care or custody for the murder or manslaughter of other children (Ref. 12). In 1994, fewer than 400 10-17 year olds were sentenced for very serious offences (under Section 53 of the Children and Young Persons Act 1993) in England and Wales.

Who is at risk?

9. Young people are more likely to be victims of personal crime than adults, older teenagers having the highest risk of being assaulted (Exhibit 7). Three-quarters of young people convicted of the most violent and serious offences and held in secure care or custody have themselves been the victim of physical, sexual or emotional abuse (Ref. 14).

Exhibit 5
Distribution of self-reported offending by 14-17 year old males in the previous 12 months

A few persistent offenders commit most of the crimes by young people.

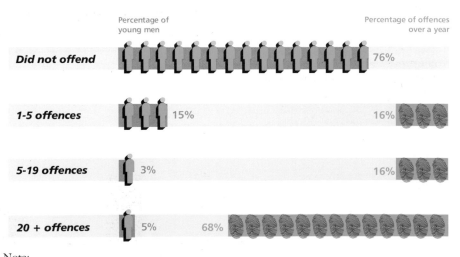

	Percentage of young men	Percentage of offences over a year
Did not offend		76%
1-5 offences	15%	16%
5-19 offences	3%	16%
20 + offences	5%	68%

Source: derived from Graham and Bowling (Ref. 9)

Note:
Assumes offenders in each of the groups commit 0, 2, 10 and 25 offences each.

Exhibit 6
Participation in self-reported offending by young people aged 14-17 years

Most offences by young people are property-related.

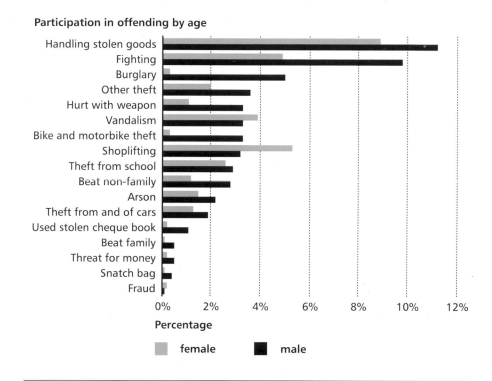

Participation in offending by age

Handling stolen goods
Fighting
Burglary
Other theft
Hurt with weapon
Vandalism
Bike and motorbike theft
Shoplifting
Theft from school
Beat non-family
Arson
Theft from and of cars
Used stolen cheque book
Beat family
Threat for money
Snatch bag
Fraud

0%   2%   4%   6%   8%   10%   12%

Percentage

female   male

Source: Graham and Bowling (Ref. 9)

Exhibit 7
Crimes experienced away from home in the last 6-8 months

Young people are more likely to be victims of personal crime than adults.

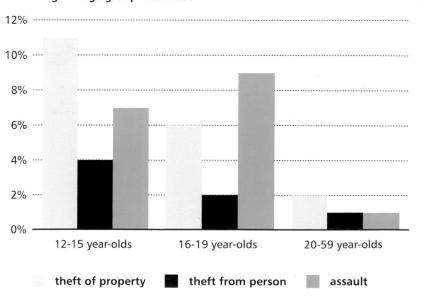

Percentage of age group victimised

12%
10%
8%
6%
4%
2%
0%

12-15 year-olds   16-19 year-olds   20-59 year-olds

theft of property   theft from person   assault

Source: British Crime Survey 1992 (Ref. 13)

Misspent Youth ...
Young People and Crime

'...over half of all burglary victims report some kind of emotional problem...'

10. Crime is concentrated on a few victims. In the 1992 British Crime Survey, 4 per cent of the victims suffered over 40 per cent, and half the victims suffered 80 per cent, of all the crimes reported (Ref. 15). The losses for victims are not only financial; over half of all burglary victims report some kind of emotional problem and almost one-quarter still experience problems six months later (Ref. 16). Similar results are emerging from the 1996 Survey (Ref.1).

11. Crime is concentrated in a few areas. People living in areas with the highest crime rates are more than ten times as likely to be the victims of personal crime, and five times as likely to suffer property crime, as those living in more law-abiding areas (Exhibit 8). Most high-crime areas are deprived, often containing large numbers of poor, single adult households with poorly supervised young people who frequently cause disturbance to other residents. The stigma of a neighbourhood in decline, with visible public disorder, reduces its relative attractiveness to prospective newcomers, further concentrating the poor and reducing the community's ability to regulate itself.

12. Children brought up in these areas are more likely to become offenders when they grow up. The risks are known to be greater for those:

- in families with inadequate parental supervision;
- with problems in school such as truancy or exclusion;
- who mix with others who offend;
- without a stable family home;
- who are not in employment or education; and
- with a heavy use of alcohol and drugs.

These risks, and ways to alleviate them, are outlined in Chapter 2.

Exhibit 8
Distribution of property and personal crime

Crime is concentrated in a few areas.

Crimes per 100 residents

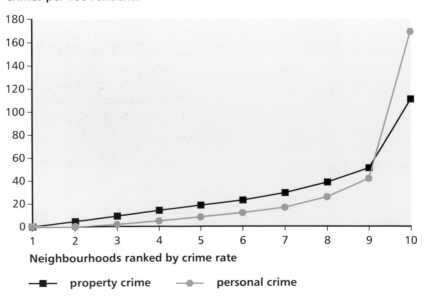

Neighbourhoods ranked by crime rate

— property crime   — personal crime

Source: Hope (Ref. 17)

Trends in youth crime

13. The Home Affairs Committee report on juvenile offenders concluded that the discrepancies between different sources of data made it difficult to draw firm conclusions as to whether offending by young people aged 10-17 years has been rising or falling over the last decade (Ref. 18). Figures published by the Home Office (Ref. 19) suggest that the number of young offenders in this age group (those cautioned by the police or found guilty in court for offences triable in a crown court) has fallen in the last decade from over 200,000 to around 150,000 (Exhibit 9).

14. The apparent fall in the rate of offending by those aged 10-17 years partly reflects demographic change; the number in this group has fallen by 16 per cent over the period. It also reflects changes to the criminal justice system, including:

◆ the reclassification by the Criminal Justice Act 1988 of three types of offence (common assault, taking a motor vehicle without consent, and criminal damage over £400 but below £2,000) from being triable in a crown court to being summary offences;

◆ the greater use of warnings for some offenders (para. 30); and

◆ a fall in the proportion of people found guilty in court.

Exhibit 9
Young people found guilty and cautioned 1983-1994

Figures published by the Home Office suggest that the number of young offenders has fallen in the last decade.

Number of young offenders (000s)

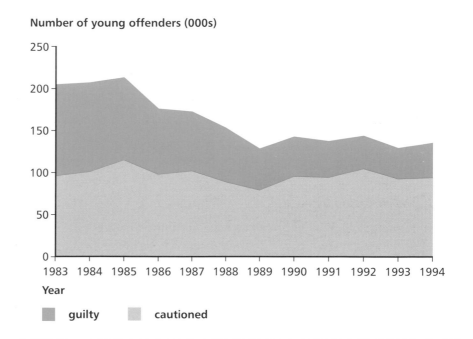

Source: Criminal Statistics (Ref. 19)

Once these factors have been taken into account, the rate of offending by young people identified by the police does not appear to have declined (Exhibit 10).

15. Moreover, young males are not growing out of offending behaviour as they used to. The known rate of offending by young adult males – aged 18 to 24 – has increased significantly, despite the changes to the criminal justice system noted above which also apply to them. As a result, the peak age of known offending has increased from 15 years in 1986 to 18 years in 1994 (Exhibit 11). The number of 18-20 year-old males is expected to grow by one-sixth over the next 10 years (Ref. 20). If no action is taken, crime committed by young adult males is likely to increase. Today's school children will be tomorrow's young adults and what happens to them now will affect their behaviour in the next few years.

Exhibit 10
Young people taken to court, cautioned and formally warned 1983-1994 per 1,000

The rate of offending by young people identified by the police appears not to have declined.

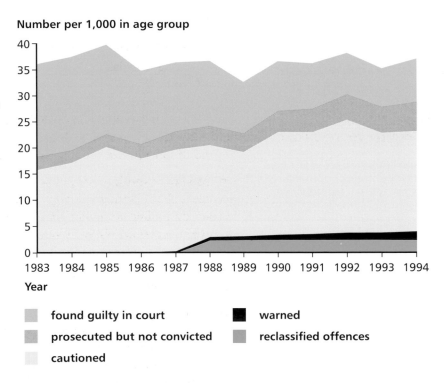

Number per 1,000 in age group

Year

found guilty in court	warned
prosecuted but not convicted	reclassified offences
cautioned	

Source: Criminal Statistics (Ref. 19); Audit Commission survey of police forces

Exhibit 11
Known offending rates in 1986 and 1994

The peak age of known offending by young men has risen from 15 years in 1986 to 18 years in 1994.

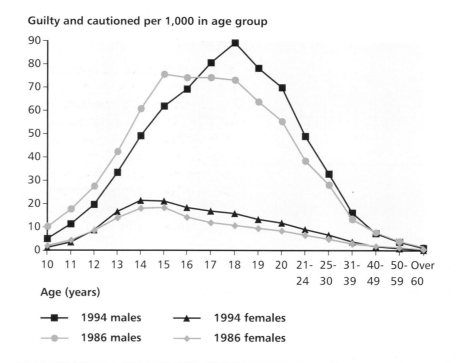

Guilty and cautioned per 1,000 in age group

Age (years)

- ■ 1994 males
- ▲ 1994 females
- ● 1986 males
- ◆ 1986 females

Source: Home Office Criminal Statistics (Ref. 19)

Dealing with antisocial behaviour by young people

'Targeting persistent offenders, to get them to change their behaviour, could have a significant effect on the overall level of youth crime.'

16. Only a small proportion of all the offences by young people are reported and recorded by the police. Just 3 per cent of offences lead to arrest and action by the criminal justice system (Exhibit 12, overleaf).

17. Moreover, much of the public concern about the behaviour of some young people is about juvenile nuisance – such as shouting and swearing, hanging about and fooling around in groups, sometimes outside other peoples' homes – rather than crime. Between one in ten and two in ten calls to the police are now about such nuisance, much of it due to young people (Ref. 21). Other people can find it distracting or intimidating – but the criminal justice system cannot help them.

18. Any strategy for tackling youth crime must consider how to address the behaviour of four different groups of young people. Targeting persistent offenders, to get them to change their behaviour, could have a significant effect on the overall level of youth crime. Young offenders who have yet to develop an entrenched pattern of offending must also be dealt with effectively; and first-time offenders must also be discouraged from becoming more deeply involved in crime. Finally, young people at risk must be discouraged from getting involved in offending in the first place.

Exhibit 12
Offending by young people and
action by the criminal justice system

Three per cent of offences lead to arrest
and action by the criminal justice system.

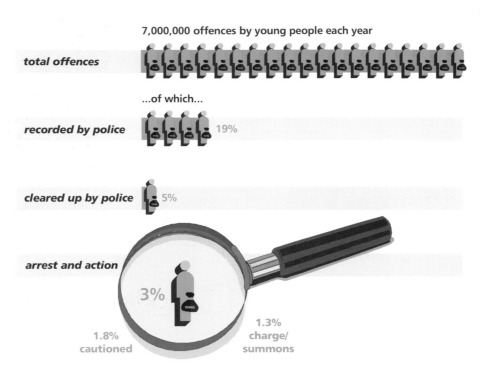

7,000,000 offences by young people each year

total offences

...of which...

recorded by police   19%

cleared up by police   5%

arrest and action

3%

1.8%
cautioned

1.3%
charge/
summons

*Sources: Criminal Statistics 1994 (Ref. 19); British
Crime Survey (Ref. 3)*

19. The immediate problem is what to do with offenders; this is the subject of
Chapter 1. Preventing offending is the subject of Chapter 2. The primary
responsibility rests with parents, who remain the most important influence on
their children, but public services can also help to guide young people towards
responsible behaviour by providing help with parenting; structured nursery
education; support in schools; positive leisure opportunities; and better
employment and training opportunities. All of this work needs to be drawn
together to form a coherent strategy at the local level. Developing such a
strategy is the subject of Chapter 3. Local authorities, in co-operation with
police authorities, should take the lead in formulating community safety plans,
identifying those neighbourhoods at greatest risk and consulting residents on
the priorities for action.

1 Tackling Offending Behaviour

Most young people known to offend receive a caution from the police, but very few of them receive any further action. The remainder are prosecuted, but half of the prosecutions are dropped or result in the young person being discharged by the court. The court process usually takes several appearances, over a period of months, before a sentencing decision is reached. The effects of different sentences on re-offending are not monitored.

The efficiency and effectiveness of the system could be improved by using 'caution plus' programmes, by reducing the time to process offenders through the court and by giving more intensive community supervision to persistent offenders. The effects of different sentences and other interventions should be monitored.

Introduction

20. When young people offend, the responsibility for identifying and dealing with them falls to a variety of central and local agencies (Exhibit 13). Of these services, the Audit Commission audits social services, probation and police forces (except the Metropolitan Police Force). This chapter examines the process for dealing with young offenders and makes recommendations for ways in which it might be improved.

21. The agencies dealing with young offenders have different views about what they are trying to achieve. The Home Office White Paper, *Protecting the Public* (Ref. 22), sets out a strategy for tackling crime, which says the Government wants and expects to see:

◆ a stronger local emphasis on preventing and reducing crime – with the newly constituted police authorities and their chief constables taking a clear lead;

◆ a co-ordinated approach to tackling crime and reducing criminality;

◆ more criminals brought to justice, targeting those who offend most frequently and cause most damage in the community;

◆ greater fairness in procedures and practice, to prevent miscarriages of justice;

◆ fewer delays in processing cases;

◆ tougher and more appropriate community sentences;

◆ sentences to deter offenders and reassure victims;

◆ mandatory sentences for certain serious crimes;

◆ greater success in preventing re-offending by convicted criminals; and

◆ better recognition of victims and attention to their needs.

Exhibit 13
Agencies in the criminal justice system for young people

The criminal justice system for young people includes a variety of central and local agencies.

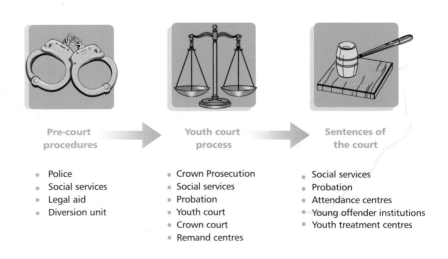

Pre-court procedures	Youth court process	Sentences of the court
• Police	• Crown Prosecution	• Social services
• Social services	• Social services	• Probation
• Legal aid	• Probation	• Attendance centres
• Diversion unit	• Youth court	• Young offender institutions
	• Crown court	• Youth treatment centres
	• Remand centres	

Source: Audit Commission

22. Most of the work with young offenders is carried out by social workers who operate under a general duty – set out in section 44 of the Children and Young Persons Act 1933 and subsequently confirmed in the Children Act 1989 – to safeguard and promote the welfare of children in need, which includes most children who offend. All of the social services departments visited were committed to diverting transient young offenders (other than serious offenders) from the criminal justice system. But few offered alternatives which tackled offending behaviour. This approach is represented in a national protocol, developed by organisations representing youth justice services (Ref. 23), which emphasises the rights and welfare needs of young offenders, as children. These different approaches need to be reconciled if agencies are to work together and fulfil their different responsibilities.

The criminal justice system for young people

23. The process for dealing with young people who offend and end up in court is complicated and may take months to complete (Exhibit 14, overleaf). Many of the processes are there to ensure that those accused of a crime are dealt with fairly and justly. In the case of young people, there are additional processes intended to ensure the welfare of the child is protected.

'Many of the processes are there to ensure that those accused of a crime are dealt with fairly and justly.'

Exhibit 14
The system for dealing with young people who offend

The process is complicated and may take months to complete.

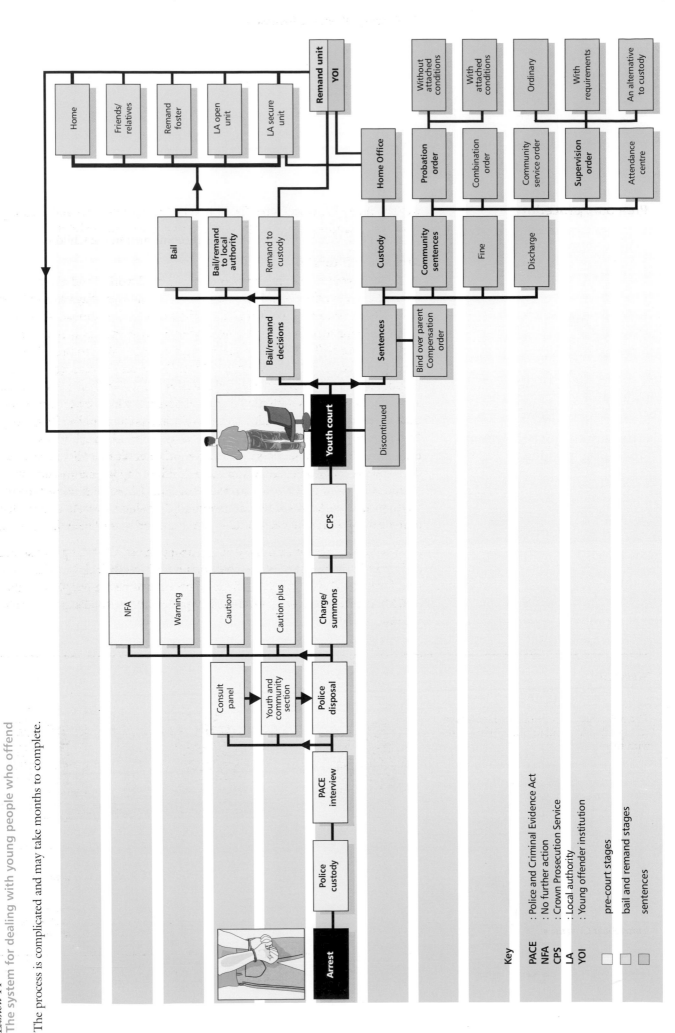

Key

PACE : Police and Criminal Evidence Act
NFA : No further action
CPS : Crown Prosecution Service
LA : Local authority
YOI : Young offender institution

☐ pre-court stages

☐ bail and remand stages

☐ sentences

Source: Audit Commission

Pre-court procedures

24. The police are responsible for identifying young offenders and deciding whether to caution or to ask the CPS to prosecute them (Exhibit 15).

Arrest and interview

25. When a young person is arrested, both a social worker and a lawyer may be needed before the police can interview them, causing delays and additional costs. If the young person is under 17, the custody officer must ask the adult responsible for them to come to the police station as soon as practicable. If they cannot or will not come, social services must be asked to provide an appropriate adult. This happens in around 30 per cent of cases (Ref. 24), at a cost of about £30 an interview, totalling around £2.7 million a year. In some areas, social services' youth justice workers spend around 10 per cent of their time acting as appropriate adults, much of it in travelling and waiting around. In other areas, social workers' time is freed up to spend on other tasks by training and using volunteers for the appropriate adult role. Social services departments that do not use volunteers to fulfil the appropriate adult role should wish to consider doing so, to free around 10 per cent of the time of youth justice workers (equivalent to around £2 million a year). Around half of this saving would be needed to recruit, train and co-ordinate the volunteers.

26. The police must inform the young person, on arrival at the police station and again in the presence of the appropriate adult, of their right to legal advice paid for by legal aid. In 1991, about 26 per cent of young people took this up (Ref. 24) at a current cost of around £100 per interview, totalling £8.5 million per year (Ref. 25).

Exhibit 15
Pre-court procedures

The police are responsible for identifying young offenders and deciding what to do with them.

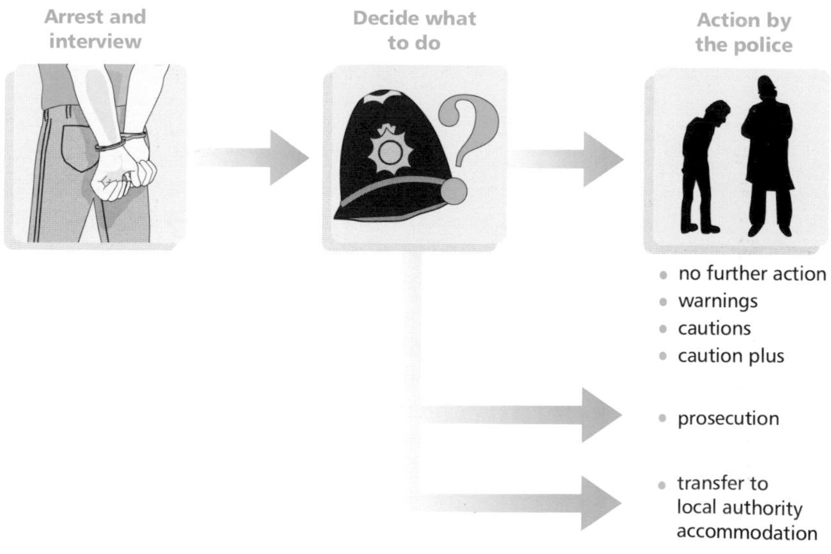

Arrest and interview	Decide what to do	Action by the police

- no further action
- warnings
- cautions
- caution plus

- prosecution

- transfer to local authority accommodation

Source: Audit Commission

'All police forces should consider whether they could use existing resources more effectively by having youth and community sections in order to liaise with other public services dealing with young people...'

Deciding what to do with the young person

27. After the interview, the police decide whether they can prove that an offence took place and, if so, what action to take. Most police forces encourage consistent decision-making by using gravity factors, which categorise offences by degrees of seriousness and identify exacerbating and mitigating factors which should be taken into account (Exhibit 16). Youth justice workers interviewed for this study supported this approach where they had been consulted in its development, and spoke of the time saved on interagency discussion. In other areas, where they had not been consulted, there was some regret at the reduction in contact between the police and themselves. Police forces that have not already done so could usefully discuss and agree gravity factors with social services, to improve consistency of decision-making and reduce the amount of interagency discussion of individual cases. Pivotal cases are referred to interagency youth panels for advice in 39 of the 43 police forces. The police, social services and a range of other services are represented, which helps to foster communication and understanding between them.

28. Most police forces have some officers responsible for youth issues, who develop expertise in the law as it affects young people and act as a contact point for other agencies dealing with young offenders. In one area visited, where the police had no such officers, the other agencies found it difficult to co-ordinate with the police, and the police were having no impact on the other agencies' policies. All police forces should consider whether they could use existing resources more effectively by having youth and community sections in order to liaise with other public services dealing with young people, notably the CPS, social services and local education authorities.

Action by the police

29. The police are unable to take action against young people under the age of 10 – the age of criminal responsibility – in England and Wales. In other cases, the police may decide to take no further action if, for instance, the young person has already been sentenced to custody or indicates that they would like the offence taken into account when another matter comes before the court.

30. The police may decide to issue a warning. Guidance issued by the Association of Chief Police Officers (ACPO) in February 1995 (Ref. 26) suggests that warnings should be given only where a formal caution is inappropriate (for example, in the case of very minor offending) or impractical. An Audit Commission survey established that 11 of the 43 forces in England and Wales – covering nearly half the population – have introduced warnings since the mid 1980s and record the number of warnings that they issue. Those records suggest that around 10 per cent of young offenders identified by the police in those areas are now warned. Current Home Office guidance (Ref. 27) says that there is no intention of inhibiting the practice of giving warnings, but makes it clear that they should not be cited in court nor recorded as a caution in the criminal statistics. So the figures for young

Exhibit 16
Examples of gravity factors

Most police forces encourage consistent decision-making by using gravity factors.

Offences	Gravity Score	Offence-specific factors	
		+	**−**
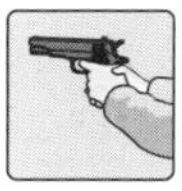 Robbery	5	Possessed weapon	Used minimum threat
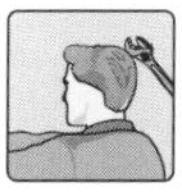 Grievous bodily harm	4	Used weapon	Provoked
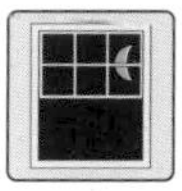 Burglary	4	Night time Occupier present Deliberately frightened occupants	Vacant premises Coerced by others
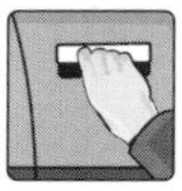 Car theft	3	Premeditated	From own family
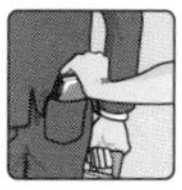 Theft	3	Planned Unrecovered property	Poverty
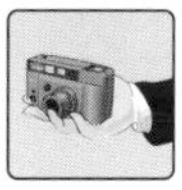 Handling	3	Property stolen to order	Under pressure
Criminal damage	3	Group offence Damage over £200	Impulsive Less than £50
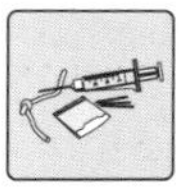 Possession of drugs	3	In prison Large quantity	Bought by group to share
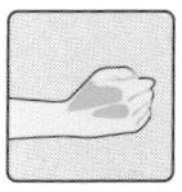 Common assault	2	Injury caused Premeditated	Impulsive action

General factors for all offences	
+	**−**
Conviction likely to result in significant sentence Offender in position of trust Offence committed while defendant on bail Offender has previous conviction or caution for comparable offence	Small or nominal penalty likely Genuine mistake or misunderstanding Offender has put right harm or loss caused Influenced by others more criminally sophisticated

Score	Action
5	Prosecute
4	Prosecute unless police decision-maker can justify not doing so
3	Pivotal
2	High probability of caution
1	Warning

Source: ACPO

offenders cautioned and found guilty which are published in *Criminal Statistics (Ref. 19)* understate the number of young offenders identified by the police.

31. Three out of five young offenders who are apprehended are cautioned, though the proportion varies around the country (Exhibit 17). A caution comprises a lecture from a police officer, usually an inspector, in the presence of a parent or other appropriate adult. It is intended to deal quickly and simply with less serious offenders, to avoid the need for appearing in court and to reduce the chances of re-offending. But police officers are not trained to issue cautions – over 90 per cent of the police officers interviewed considered that they should be. Police officers cautioning a young person could ask parents to encourage the young person to write a letter of apology to the victim and, if appropriate, pass it on. But no example of this being done was observed by the Commission.

32. Cautioning works well for first offenders, and seven out of ten are not known to re-offend within two years (Ref. 27). But it becomes progressively less effective once a pattern of offending sets in. The more offences that have been committed, the higher the probability that the offender will be caught re-offending in the future. So a key decision is how soon to intervene to address the offending behaviour. The evidence suggests that, after three occasions, prosecution is more effective in reducing re-offending than a caution (Exhibit 18). Home Office guidance indicates that one caution is appropriate before prosecution in court, unless the subsequent offence is trivial, or sufficient time has elapsed since the first offence to suggest that it had some effect (Ref. 28). But some young people are cautioned twice or more without further action being taken. Unlike warnings, previous cautions may be cited in court. But police records of previous cautions are often incomplete, so citing previous cautions is unreliable and inconsistent. In one area visited,

Exhibit 17
Caution v being taken to court in different police force areas

Most young people known to offend receive a caution, though the proportion varies around the country.

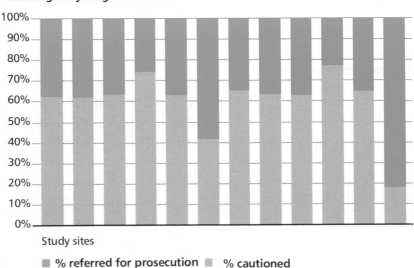

Percentage of young offenders

Study sites

■ % referred for prosecution   ■ % cautioned

Source: Home Office Criminal Statistics Supplementary Tables

Exhibit 18
Re-offending after successive
cautions and prosecutions

After three occasions, prosecution is
more effective in reducing re-offending
than a caution.

*Source: Inspector B Harrison, West Yorkshire
Police*

Probability of re-offending

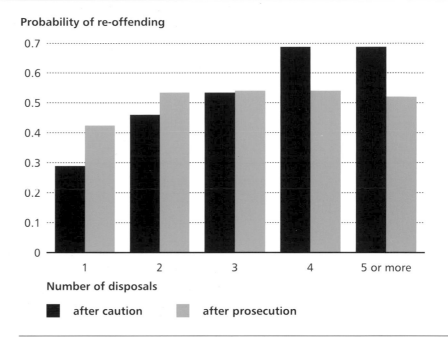

Number of disposals

■ after caution   ■ after prosecution

consistency was achieved by not mentioning cautions at all in the youth court.

33. Few young people who are cautioned receive any other intervention or service, sometimes called 'caution plus' (Exhibit 19). At only two of the 12 sites visited were local agencies addressing the behaviour of significant numbers of young people cautioned by the police. Elsewhere, agencies were either opposed in principle to addressing offending behaviour outside the court system or the co-ordination between them was inadequate.

Exhibit 19
Use of caution plus for young
offenders

Few young people who are cautioned
receive any other intervention or service.

Source: Audit Commission site visits

Study sites

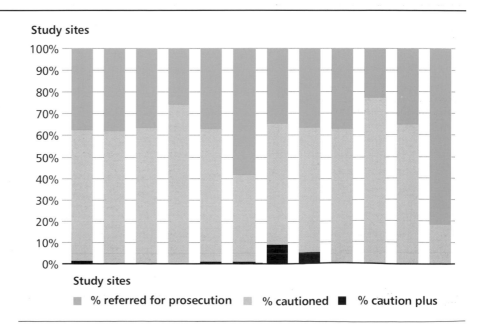

Study sites

■ % referred for prosecution   ■ % cautioned   ■ % caution plus

Prosecution

34. The police start proceedings against two out of every five young offenders. But prosecuting them through the courts is not particularly efficient. Police officers must first complete around 40 forms to process a young offender – illustrated in the Audit Commission report, *Helping with Enquiries* (Ref. 29). Police officers interviewed in 1995 suggested that once a young person was brought to a police station it took, on average, four to five hours to arrange and conduct an interview and complete the required paperwork. The details vary from force to force, but the police continue to struggle with mountains of paper – which cover force-wide and central statistical collection, procedures connected to tapes of interviews and other evidence, as well as papers to support the prosecution case.

35. The paperwork needed by the Crown Prosecution Service (CPS) and the courts is considerable, to be sure that there is sufficient evidence to supplement any prosecution case, and is often not completed to the timetable and quality standards they require. A Trials Issues Group – including representatives from the CPS, the police, the courts, the Lord Chancellor's Department and the Home Office – recommended in 1994 that in cases expected to result in a guilty plea in a magistrates court, the files prepared for these cases should be reduced to:

- typed witness statements to establish every element of each alleged offence;
- eyewitness statements where the accused is charged with actual bodily harm or assault with intent to resist arrest;
- the accused's list of convictions;
- the victim's compensation claim; and
- for a trial period of a year, a typed short descriptive note of admissions, mitigating and aggravating factors disclosed by the defendant when interviewed by the police.

Fuller files are required where a not guilty plea is anticipated. A recent Home Office review found that police forces operating this system submitted only 60 per cent of files to the CPS within the agreed time guidelines, with only 45 per cent submitted to the agreed quality standards (Ref. 30). Police forces could make more effective use of their officers' time by simplifying the internal paperwork required for dealing with young people. Interview summaries forwarded to the CPS should be kept brief, with a copy of the relevant tape made available if more information is needed by the CPS or defence lawyers.

Transfers to local authority accommodation

36. After young people are interviewed or charged by the police, they are usually released on police bail. If the police decide not to grant bail, a young person under 17 should, by law, be transferred to local authority accommodation – unless the custody officer certifies that no local authority secure accommodation is available and the use of any other local authority accommodation would be inadequate to protect the public from serious harm. In some areas, the police will not transfer young people of 12 years or more to

'Around one-quarter of prosecutions against young people are discontinued by the CPS or dismissed by the court...'

local authorities unless a secure bed is available, so children as young as 12 are kept in a police cell for a night or weekend (Ref. 31). In other areas, young people transferred by the police to local authorities are sometimes allowed to walk away, either because social workers have difficulty finding accommodation for them or because they feel unable to restrain them. This frequently leads to a waste of police time in re-arresting the same people. The Department of Health has issued guidance which makes clear that local authorities are expected to take positive action to prevent a child leaving a home without permission (Ref. 32). Social services should ensure that they have suitable accommodation for young people transferred to them by the police until they can appear in court. Guidance to social workers on what to do if the young person starts to leave the accommodation should be agreed with the police.

Cases withdrawn, discontinued and dismissed

37. Once the police have decided to prosecute a young person, they start proceedings by charging them or prompting the court to issue a summons. The CPS then decides whether or not to prosecute the case, taking into account the evidence available and the public interest. Around one-quarter of prosecutions against young people are discontinued by the CPS or dismissed by the court for one reason or another (Exhibit 20). The precise proportion is unclear because some cases are merged and some charges are dropped, to be replaced with others. But:

♦ an Audit Commission survey of 103 young offenders, who were either on supervision orders or released on licence from custody, found that they recalled 22 per cent of all prosecutions against them being dropped;

♦ a survey by the CPS in one area of the country found that 14 per cent of cases against juveniles were discontinued, with a further 11 per cent dismissed (Ref. 33); and

♦ figures published in *Criminal Statistics* show that in 1994, 31 per cent of proceedings at youth courts for all offences were either discontinued or withdrawn and a further 7 per cent were dismissed.

Exhibit 20
Young offenders prosecuted and found guilty

Around one-quarter of prosecutions against young people are discontinued or dismissed for one reason or another.

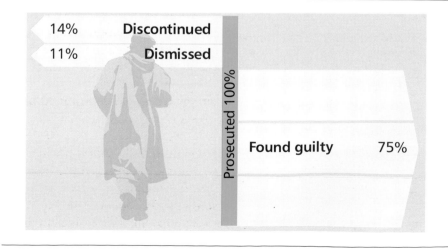

Source: Crown Prosecution Service survey in West Midlands 1996

Most cases which are discontinued or withdrawn by the CPS – 88 per cent in 1991 – appear in court at least once (Ref. 34), which can waste the time of those attending court, including social services and probation.

38. Young offenders interviewed for this report who had prosecutions dropped were not aware of the reasons why, and commented on the apparently arbitrary nature of the system. At the sites visited, cautions were rarely given by the police if the CPS decided not to prosecute, despite guilt being admitted – though this problem may be reduced following guidance on cautioning issued by ACPO at the end of 1995, which encourages police forces to caution in these circumstances. Police forces should ensure that offenders are cautioned where guilt is admitted but cases have been discontinued.

The youth court process

39. The youth court continues the process of identifying young people who offend. It makes decisions about remanding young people between court appearances, whether they offended and, if so, what should be done with them (Exhibit 21).

40. Prosecution through the court is expensive, costing around £2,500 on average per person sentenced by the court (Ref. 35). Many of the cases processed through the youth courts involve fighting between young people who know each other, or the theft of goods worth only a few pounds. There are at least five paid officials in the youth court – a magistrates' clerk, a crown prosecutor, a defence lawyer (paid from legal aid), an usher and one or more officers from youth justice services and probation (Exhibit 22) – plus the magistrates, a parent and the young person. Police officers do not attend the youth court unless asked to appear as witnesses. Refinements introduced to the criminal justice system in recent years, such as advance disclosure (under which the prosecution has to copy relevant papers to the defence lawyer before any case is presented in court), are being applied to all youth court cases, making the system slow and expensive.

Exhibit 21
Youth court process

Decisions are made in the youth court about remanding young people between court appearances, whether they offended and, if so, what should be done with them.

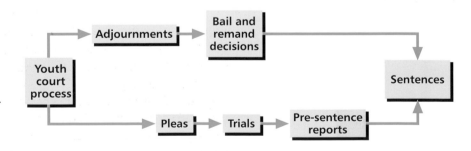

Source: Audit Commission

Exhibit 22
People in the youth court

There are at least five paid officials in the youth court plus the magistrates, a parent and the young person.

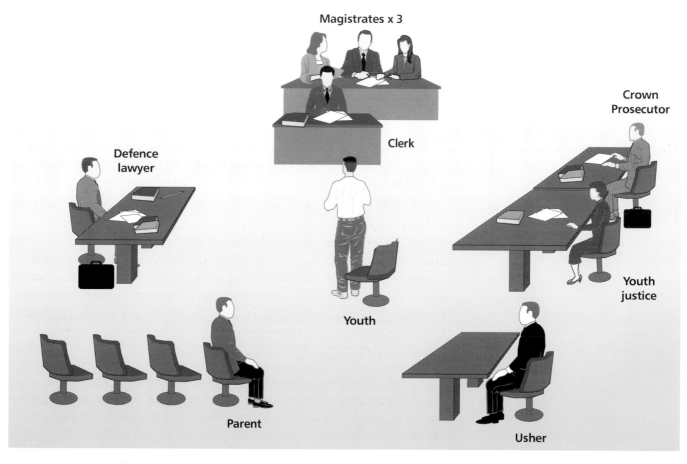

Source: Audit Commission

Youth justice and probation services

41. The court looks for advice on young people to youth justice or probation services. Youth justice services emerged as distinct parts of social services departments during the 1980s. About one-third of youth justice workers' time is spent addressing offending behaviour – working with offenders on caution plus, bail support, supervision orders and those released on licence from custody (Exhibit 23, overleaf) – while most of the remainder is spent helping the police and the youth court. Staff reported that they felt distant from other social services for children, making it difficult for them to respond to the welfare needs of the young people they deal with. In one area visited services to the youth court were delivered by social workers in area teams, but the courts were unhappy with their lack of knowledge of the requirements of the court. Two others had located youth justice alongside other social services for children, in geographically related children's resource centres. The service

Exhibit 23
How social services youth justice workers spend their time

One-third of youth justice workers' time is spent addressing offending behaviour, while most of the remainder is spent helping the police and the youth court.

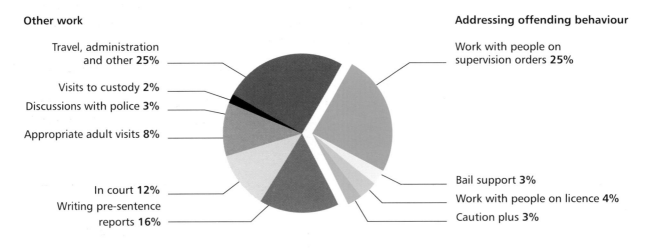

Other work

Travel, administration and other **25%**

Visits to custody **2%**

Discussions with police **3%**

Appropriate adult visits **8%**

In court **12%**

Writing pre-sentence reports **16%**

Addressing offending behaviour

Work with people on supervision orders **25%**

Bail support **3%**

Work with people on licence **4%**

Caution plus **3%**

Source: sample of 60 youth justice workers at Audit Commission study sites

providers were encouraged to identify the individual needs of the young people, while the centre managers decided how best to meet those needs within the resources available.

42. Probation provides the same service to youth courts. The split of responsibilities between probation and social services is negotiated locally by the services themselves, so different arrangements exist throughout England and Wales. In most areas, social services deal with all young people in court aged 10-15 and those aged 16 already known to them, while probation deals with any others aged 16 and all those aged 17. But only 3 per cent of offenders supervised by probation in England and Wales are under 18 when sentenced by the courts (Ref. 36). The split of responsibility can lead to duplication of services, with officers from both services sitting in the same court, fulfilling the same function. In two of the 12 sites visited, integrated social services and probation teams dealt with all cases in the youth court, thus removing duplication. Such teams operate in 20 per cent of local authorities in England and Wales (Ref. 37). Social services should consider, with the local probation service, whether to form joint youth justice service teams.

Adjournments

43. The youth court process is often complex and lengthy. Four out of five youth court cases observed by the Audit Commission were adjourned – often because the young person was not present, or to commission a pre-sentence report (PSR); or because the defence lawyer had not been briefed, or legal aid had not been sorted out (Exhibit 24). On average, a young person appears in the youth court four times in the course of one case (Exhibit 25, overleaf), although this varies considerably between areas.

44. On average, the whole process can take from 70 days in some areas to 170 days in others (Exhibit 26, overleaf). It takes up much of the time of youth justice workers, lawyers and witnesses, including police officers – adding to their costs. It also means a long delay between a young person's arrest and sentence, which makes any punishment less meaningful.

Exhibit 24
Reasons for adjourning youth court appearances

Four out of five youth court cases were adjourned.

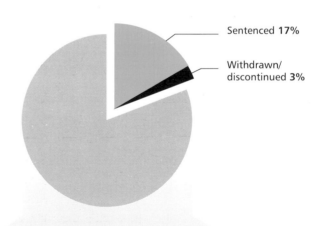

Sentenced **17%**

Withdrawn/
discontinued **3%**

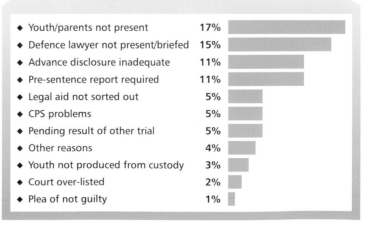

79% of cases adjourned because:

◆ Youth/parents not present	17%	
◆ Defence lawyer not present/briefed	15%	
◆ Advance disclosure inadequate	11%	
◆ Pre-sentence report required	11%	
◆ Legal aid not sorted out	5%	
◆ CPS problems	5%	
◆ Pending result of other trial	5%	
◆ Other reasons	4%	
◆ Youth not produced from custody	3%	
◆ Court over-listed	2%	
◆ Plea of not guilty	1%	

Source: Audit Commission analysis of 200 youth court appearances

Exhibit 25
Number of appearances for an offence

On average, a young person appears in the youth court four times in the course of one case...

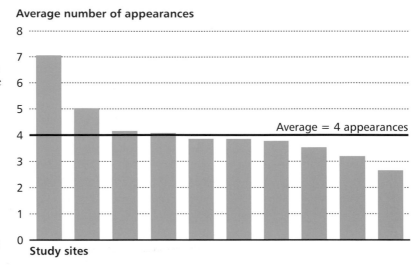

Average number of appearances

Average = 4 appearances

Study sites

Source: Audit Commission survey of 600 sentenced young offenders

Exhibit 26
Average number of days between arrest and sentence by site

...and, on average, the whole process can take from 70 days in some areas to 170 days in others.

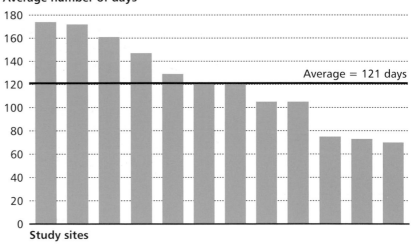

Average number of days

Average = 121 days

Study sites

Source: Audit Commission survey of 600 sentenced young offenders

Bail and remand decisions

45. In between court appearances, most young people are remanded on unconditional bail and may return home (Exhibit 27) – so some of them continue offending while they go through the lengthy court process. One-third of 359 young people bailed in Gloucestershire in 1994 re-offended on bail, with 40 per cent of the offences committed after they had spent more than three months on bail. One solution is to speed up the court process. Another is for local authorities to provide activities to occupy the time of defendants with nothing to do, as in South East Kent (Box A). Eighty-eight per cent of social service departments now provide some bail support services for young people (Ref. 38). The Wandsworth Bail Support service, run by the

Exhibit 27
Remand status of 600 offenders at sentence

In between court appearances, most young people are remanded on unconditional bail.

Number of young offenders

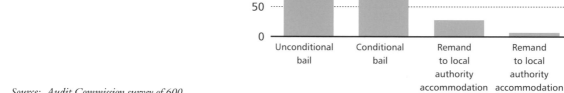

Source: Audit Commission survey of 600 sentenced young offenders

Royal Philanthropic Society, costs around £100 a week, which compares well with around £600 a week for local authority residential care and £1,000 for placement in the private or voluntary sector. Social services departments that do not provide a bail support service should consider doing so.

46. Other young people are locked up on remand, either in prison establishments – where some are confined to small cells for over 20 hours a day (Ref. 39) – or in local authority secure accommodation. These options are costly. At the end of March 1996, 779 15-17 year olds were in prison custody

Box A
South East Kent Bail Support Scheme

The scheme is offered as a condition of bail to all those under 18 years who risk having bail refused. It aims to satisfy the courts that remand to custody or local authority accommodation is unnecessary, provided the young person complies with the rules and requirements of the scheme, and to offer appropriate control within the community.

The scheme offers structured activity, with responsible adults supervising, from noon to 3.30pm on four days a week. Staff offer help with basic skills, including budgeting and the preparation of a meal, and encourage self-discipline. A laundry and shower are available. Structured sessions include job seeking, careers advice and further education opportunities; supervised sport; information on drug and alcohol abuse, sex education, housing and welfare issues; and practical skills, such as form filling and changing a plug. Young people are regularly reminded of the very serious consequences of re-offending for themselves, their families and the victims of crime. If a young person fails to attend or behaves badly, a youth justice worker decides whether to inform the police that the bail conditions have been breached. The scheme costs approximately £10,000 a year and can deal with up to seven young people at one time.

on remand and unsentenced – 20 per cent more than the year before. This group accounted for 38 per cent of all 15-17 year olds in prison. Although rudimentary education is provided to those under 16, a prison visitors' report from one of the major young offender institutions suggests that the minimum legal requirements of 15 hours a week for prisoners of school age are not being met (Ref. 40). The Commission's survey of 600 sentenced young offenders found that over one-third of those remanded in custody who were subsequently found guilty were not given a custodial sentence. Some remands can be avoided, and resources saved, by the use of intensive support for those on bail. While extra costs fall on local authority social services, they would be offset by savings to the prison service, requiring some transfer of resources.

47. Young people remanded to local authority accommodation or to custody have to be produced in court every seven days unless and until their cases are committed to the Crown Court. These appearances disrupt any education or behavioural programmes in which the young person might be engaged, and cost significant sums of money for escort staff and transport. One case in 1995 cost a local authority £7,200 to transport a young person to and from court on 19 occasions, plus £64,000 for secure accommodation for 216 days. The Criminal Procedure and Investigations Act 1996 includes a provision to allow courts to remand people for up 28 days on a second and subsequent court appearance, which should help reduce the extra costs incurred by social services when it is implemented.

48. A further 70 young people are held on remand in local authority secure units. Local authority secure units charge between £1,800 and £3,450 a week (Exhibit 28) – those in London, where secure accommodation is in short supply, charging appreciably more than others. The costs are paid by the social services department responsible for the young person. Some secure

Exhibit 28
Comparative cost of one week's placement at...

Local authority secure units charge between £1,800 and £3,450 a week.

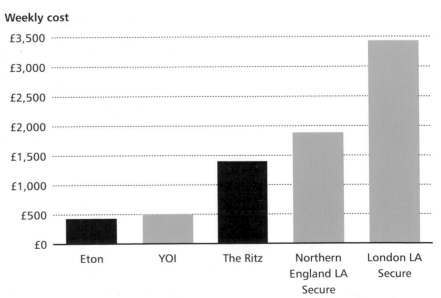

Weekly cost

Source: Audit Commission, individual establishments

'Local authority secure units should be able to identify their costs and charge fees sufficient to cover them.'

units share facilities with open units and have no clear rules for allocating costs between them. Others visited had made surpluses which were surrendered to the parent authority. Local authority secure units should be able to identify their costs and charge fees sufficient to cover them.

Pleas

49. The proportion of young people pleading guilty in court has fallen from 65 per cent in 1989 to 55 per cent in 1994 (Exhibit 29), adding to costs for the police – who have to prepare fuller files where the plea is not guilty. Pleas submitted by adults have changed similarly (Ref. 42). The legal aid fee structure introduced in 1993, which pays lawyers more if their clients plead not guilty, may contribute to the problem. The Government's proposals for contracting criminal legal aid by area could help to remove any perverse incentive of this sort (Ref. 43) in the future.

Trials

50. Most young offenders still plead guilty, making a trial unnecessary. In some cases, they change an initial plea of not guilty to guilty if the prosecution witnesses attend for a trial. This is one of the reasons why most of the trials arranged in the youth court collapse (Exhibit 30, overleaf). The results include wasted expenditure by the police: 60 per cent of police officers who attend court to give evidence leave without having done so (Ref. 44). Although most trials collapse for reasons outside the immediate control of the court, such as key individuals not attending, courts tend to over-list to avoid wasting their time. This does not, however, save the time of other agencies or witnesses, so

Exhibit 29
Pleas in the youth court

The proportion of young people pleading guilty in court has fallen.

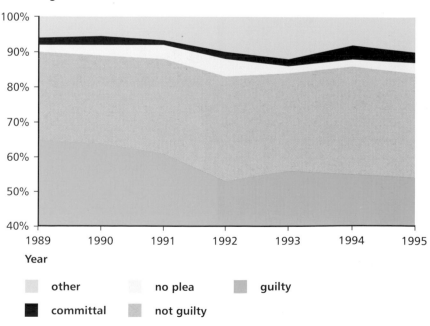

Percentage of defendants

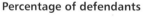

Source: Lord Chancellor's Department (Ref. 41)

Exhibit 30
An analysis of 700 youth court trials

Most of the trials arranged in the youth court collapse.

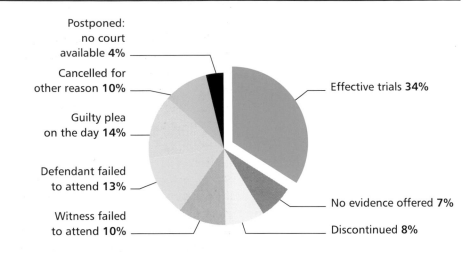

Postponed: no court available **4%**

Cancelled for other reason **10%**

Guilty plea on the day **14%**

Defendant failed to attend **13%**

Witness failed to attend **10%**

Effective trials **34%**

No evidence offered **7%**

Discontinued **8%**

Source: Inner London Youth Court

some youth courts use pre-trial reviews which ensure that the defence and prosecution are ready to begin the trial on the due date. These reviews can improve the estimates of trial length and minimise the occasions that victims, police, other witnesses and social services attend court without being needed. Youth courts should consider piloting pre-trial reviews, to establish their effectiveness in reducing the time wasted by people who attend court for trials that do not take place.

Pre-sentence reports

51. The courts may commission a PSR from either the youth justice or probation service, to help their decision-making. The process can be hampered by the time it can take for the necessary CPS papers to reach the PSR author. One site found that this transfer of documents took from five to 20 working days. At some sites, the CPS regularly sends all the files to the probation service, even though the youth justice service prepares the majority of the PSRs. However, national standards, issued jointly by the Home Office, Department of Health and Welsh Office (Ref. 45), require PSR authors to make contact with the offender within two days of the report being commissioned. If the papers have not arrived, the author has to rely on the offender, and any notes taken by youth justice in court, for a description of the offence. The CPS could help to expedite cases through the youth court by passing papers needed for PSRs directly to the service preparing the report.

52. The majority of officers writing PSRs have completed a two-year diploma course in social work of which, typically, a four-week option covers offending behaviour, though from April 1997 the probation service will accept staff with an NVQ in social work. When asked about what they recommended in pre-sentence reports, few authors of PSRs referred to published evidence on what is known to work in reducing re-offending. All staff involved in the preparation of PSRs should have the appropriate skills and knowledge and receive appropriate training and supervision.

'Youth justice services should canvass magistrates' views on the value of the PSRs that they provide each year – more often if the magistrates wish.'

53. Probation services, and some, but not all, youth justice services, regularly seek magistrates' views on the usefulness of the pre-sentence reports they produce. National standards (Ref. 45) state that chief probation officers and directors of social services should ensure that there is effective liaison with sentencers to provide information on the work of the team, give feedback on individual progress and encourage an informed dialogue. Youth justice services should canvass magistrates' views on the value of the PSRs that they provide each year – more often if the magistrates wish.

Speeding up the process

54. Costs would be reduced, and young offenders dealt with more effectively, if the court process were completed more quickly. Although courts are given targets and financial incentives to process cases expeditiously, the other agencies and professionals are not. In some areas, youth justice services are not even invited to attend youth court user groups. Youth court user groups for all agencies involved in the youth court, including youth justice services, should meet regularly and agree local targets for the average number of days it should take, from arrest, for a young person to be sentenced by the youth court.

Sentences of the court

55. Surprisingly, little or nothing happens to half of the young people proceeded against by the police. One out of four cases is withdrawn, discontinued or dismissed (para. 37) – because the young person is innocent; or the evidence is insufficient; or because CPS consider it would not be in the public interest to proceed with the case. A further one out of four is given a conditional or absolute discharge (Exhibit 31, overleaf).

Reducing re-offending

56. Current arrangements do little to punish most young offenders identified by the police. Do they help to reduce re-offending? Research – summarised in Appendix 1 – indicates that programmes which reduce re-offending by persistent offenders most effectively:

- are based on behaviour and skills training;
- help individuals into employment or school;
- involve interventions of six months or more, with at least two contacts per week and/or more than 100 total contact hours;
- are community-based, because it is easier to relate lessons learned to real life;
- have consistent aims and methods;
- are delivered by well-trained and skilled practitioners; and
- are carefully matched to the offender's needs (Refs. 46, 47).

Exhibit 31
Disposals received by young people
prosecuted for offences

One out of four cases is withdrawn,
discontinued or dismissed and a further one
out of four is given a discharge.

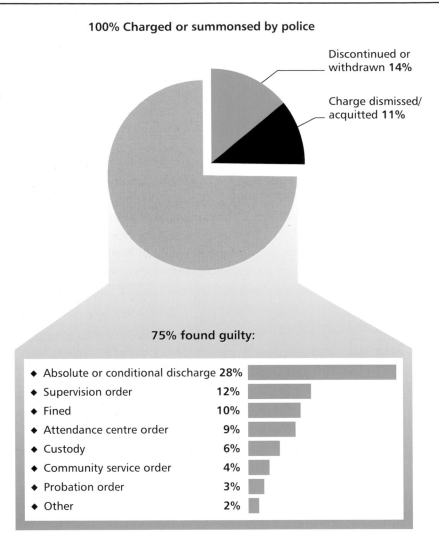

100% Charged or summonsed by police

Discontinued or
withdrawn **14%**

Charge dismissed/
acquitted **11%**

75% found guilty:

◆ Absolute or conditional discharge **28%**	
◆ Supervision order	**12%**
◆ Fined	**10%**
◆ Attendance centre order	**9%**
◆ Custody	**6%**
◆ Community service order	**4%**
◆ Probation order	**3%**
◆ Other	**2%**

Source: Crown Prosecution Service 1996; Criminal Statistics 1994

57. Approaches which tend to be ineffective with the most persistent group are:

◆ general counselling, casework, family counselling and psycho-dynamic therapy – which may improve self-esteem but do not reduce antisocial behaviour;

◆ unstructured groups – potentially fostering communications which reinforce offending behaviour; and

◆ exclusively punishment-based programmes – which tend to harden attitudes, without causing offenders to reflect on their behaviour. If punishment is to have a substantial effect on subsequent behaviour, it needs to be immediate, comprehensible to the individual and should show the way to alternative ways of behaving (Ref. 46).

58. Individuals at higher risk of re-offending, including persistent offenders, are usually found to be more influenced by intensive programmes (Refs. 47, 48), but low-risk individuals often do better with less intensive programmes.

Psychologists have a tradition of research and evaluation, but none is employed in probation or youth justice services in England and Wales. These services could usefully consider how the knowledge and expertise of psychologists, among other disciplines, can be used to help devise, implement and monitor behavioural and cognitive-behavioural programmes in community settings.

Fines, compensation orders and binding over

59. The youth court can order young offenders or their parents to pay fines or compensation. The Criminal Justice Act 1991 gave the courts duties to order parents or guardians of young offenders under 16 to pay fines, compensation and costs, unless they consider that unreasonable. In practice, few parents are fined, despite the Criminal Justice Act 1991 (Exhibit 32), often because the parents lack the means to pay. Use of fines has been falling steadily in recent years. Fewer than one in three young offenders are ordered to pay compensation (Ref. 49).

60. The Criminal Justice Act 1991 also gave the courts a duty to bind over the parents of offenders aged 10-15 or to give reasons in court for not doing do, and a power to bind over parents of offenders aged 16-17, for up to £1,000. However, none of the magistrates, clerks and police officers interviewed was clear as to how bindovers could be enforced. Since police officers are not informed when parents are bound over, they can do little. The Justices Clerks' Society and Magistrates' Association issued guidance on 30 September which may clarify matters (Ref. 50).

Exhibit 32
Fines for under 18s

Few parents of young offenders are fined, despite the Criminal Justice Act 1991.

Source: Criminal Statistics 1994

Number of cases (000s)

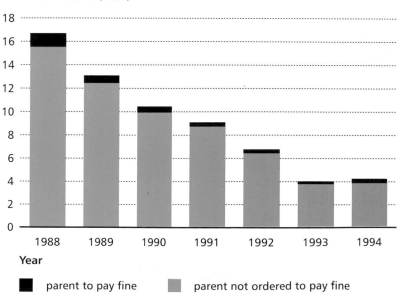

Attendance centre orders

61. Attendance centre orders usually require the young person to attend centres run by off-duty police officers on a Saturday morning. There is no published evaluation of these centres.

Supervision orders

62. Most supervision orders are overseen by a youth justice worker, though probation officers are responsible for around 30 per cent. Young people serving supervision orders said that they generally meet their supervising officers for around an hour a week for the first three months, then fortnightly or less for the remainder of the order, often discussing personal problems such as benefit claims, efforts to arrange training or employment, housing issues and personal relationships. The priority, so far as youth justice workers were concerned, was to form a good relationship with the young offenders. So the general picture is of fairly low-intensity, often unstructured, contact (Exhibit 33). This level of contact is more intensive than for most sentences issued by the court but considerably less than research suggests is needed in order to be effective with persistent offenders (see Appendix 1). But intensive work costs money, so putting this approach into practice could mean identifying savings elsewhere in the system.

63. A court may insert requirements into an order to require the young person:

♦ to attend at a specified place at specified times;

♦ to take part in various activities; and/or

♦ to live at a particular place.

Alternatively, the court may delegate authority to the supervising officer to require the offender to do any of these things. Specified activities imposed by a supervision order sometimes make use of projects in which offending behaviour is addressed and a high level of commitment is required from the young person. Although the availability of these projects varies in different parts of the country, some are under-used. At one site an expensive community project, whose capital costs were paid by City Challenge money from central government, was running at less than one-third of capacity, while many young offenders received general supervision orders and others went to custody. This is a waste of valuable resources (Box B, p40). Youth justice services and probation should ensure that good use is made of publicly funded facilities that are intended to address offending behaviour by young people, by discussing with magistrates in youth court user groups the sort of young people who would benefit from them. Where transport links allow, it may make sense for projects to offer to take young people from neighbouring areas.

Exhibit 33
Time spent with supervising officer on a supervision order

The general picture is of fairly low-intensity contact – considerably less than research suggests is needed to be effective with persistent offenders.

Frequency of seeing supervising officer

Youths on supervision orders

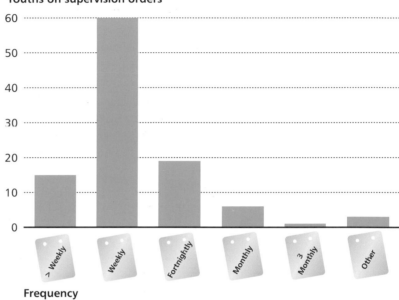

Frequency

Length of time with supervising officer

Youths on supervision orders

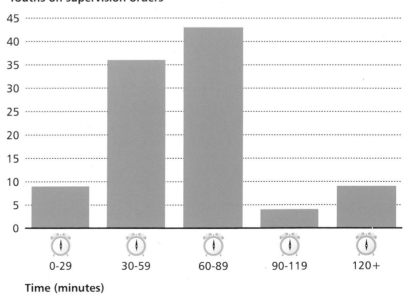

Time (minutes)

Source: Audit Commission survey of 103 young people on supervision orders

This project provides activities for young people aged 14-25 who are expected to attend four days a week for 30 or 60 days. The initial costs were paid by City Challenge. Current funding is provided by social services, probation and NCH Action for Children, which runs the project. Young people who arrive a minute late are not admitted to a session. If they miss more than two sessions, they are taken back to court for breaching the order. Five compulsory modules cover:

- **offending behaviour:** What are the antecedents, behaviour and consequences (ABC) of offending behaviour? Links are drawn between an individual's experience of being a victim and his or her offending behaviour;

- **social skills:** relationships, communications, assertiveness, contraception;

- **numeracy and literacy:** leading to a stage of a City and Guilds certificate;

- **job search:** for those over 17. Younger offenders undertake education; and

- **substance abuse and HIV:** providing information on drug abuse.

Further options cover information technology, basic word processing, art and design, constructive use of leisure time, cookery and living skills.

Over the first 19 months, the project assessed around 190 young offenders. Of the 166 who were considered likely to benefit, only 38 (23 per cent) ended up on the project. The others were dealt with as follows; either because PSR authors recommended a lower level of intervention than the project or the courts decided that a custodial sentence was appropriate:

custody	34
probation order	29
supervision order	15
community service order	19
combination order	12
attendance centre order	2
fine	1
conditional discharge	3
decision awaited	13
NCH for Action project	38
Total	**166**

As a result, the project runs at about a quarter of its capacity of 24 young people, and at more than twice the £1,100 cost per place implied by full capacity. So valuable resources focused on addressing offending behaviour are being poorly used.

'Several imaginative projects use mentors to support and encourage young people at risk of offending or experiencing other difficulties.'

64. Persistent offenders should receive more intensive supervision in the community, with programmes that draw on the research about which approaches work. Probation services often have more experience with supervision of this kind and could contribute their knowledge as full members where teams are integrated.

65. Several imaginative projects use mentors to support and encourage young people at risk of offending or experiencing other difficulties (Box C). Some of the schemes used older role models, while others use young people as mentors. Youth justice services should consider using mentoring schemes for those on supervision orders, to give the young offender support and encouragement in addressing their behaviour. Motor projects, which are available in some areas, can provide appropriate ways to change the behaviour of persistent car or motorbike offenders (Box D, overleaf).

Other community sentences

66. Probation orders, community service orders or combination orders may be imposed on offenders aged 16 or 17, following the Criminal Justice Act 1991. These orders must be overseen in part or whole by a probation officer,

Box C
The Dalston Youth Project, Hackney

This project is aimed at vulnerable young people aged between 15 and 19, who may be referred by anyone: the police, youth workers, social workers, schools or friends. In practice, 80 per cent are known to have offended and 60 per cent have been excluded from school. Over 60 per cent are black. Attendance is voluntary.

After an initial meeting, the most vulnerable young people are selected for a residential course, which is a mix of outdoor challenge, reflecting on their lives and setting goals for the future. On return, they are matched with a mentor, whom they see every week, meet as a group every month and take part in a range of educational programmes. These can include 'taster' courses at the local college, basic education in literacy and numeracy, job-shadowing placements and careers advice.

The mentors are volunteers drawn from the local community, identified by advertising and word of mouth. Some drop out when they find out more about what is involved, others drop out during training and a few are not selected. Overall, one in three of those who come forward eventually become a mentor. Most are in their late 20s and are similar in background and ethnicity to the young people on the project. They receive intensive training and regular back-up support, individually and in groups.

The programme, which costs around £3,000 per young person, is funded by social services, City Challenge and private trusts. Of the 26 young people who participated in the first year's programme, 77 per cent of those who had been offenders went on to a college training course or to paid employment, as did 71 per cent of those who had previously been excluded from school. During the programme, offending by known offenders on the project dropped by 61 per cent, compared with the year before they joined.

Box D
The BUMPY Project, Kirklees

This scheme was begun by a police constable in the early 1980s, in response to the high level of theft of motorbikes in the area. It was begun with charitable fundraising and now has a variety of sources of income, including contracts with probation and social services, City Challenge, and trusts and fees from courses for the general public. Young people who are not offenders may also attend the BUMPY project, so it is not contingent on being convicted of an offence.

The aim is to teach young people to ride safely, in a controlled environment where riding is off the road and legal, and to provide courses in motorbike mechanics which can lead to an NVQ qualification. Forty per cent of the users of the project are young offenders who attend as part of their supervision or probation order, usually for between 36 and 60 hours over an eight-week period. They must commit themselves to the full programme and are suspended and referred back to the supervising officer and the court for non-attendance. They may continue the course after their sentence has been completed if they wish. The offender programmes also include sessions on offending behaviour and understanding the victim's point of view. The cost of a 36-hour supervision programme is £252 and that of a 60-hour programme is £444. Forty-eight per cent of motor offenders do not re-offend within a year of leaving the project. Among those who do re-offend, 90 per cent do so less frequently and less seriously than they did before they joined the programme.

although they do not differ significantly from a supervision order with specified activities. In principle, this overlapping jurisdiction for 16 and 17 year olds gives the court discretion to sentence according to the maturity of the individual. But, in practice, magistrates depend upon the authors of PSRs for advice on sentencing. Which agency writes the report depends, in turn, on bilateral agreements between the youth justice and probation services, and the service which writes the report generally oversees any community order.

Custody

67. The use of custodial sentences for 10-17 year olds has fallen in recent years: from two per thousand in 1984 to one per thousand in 1994 (Exhibit 34). The average length of these sentences is also shorter: 95 per cent of custodial sentences on young people are now for less than a year (Ref. 51), with an average of five months. But the re-conviction figures are worst for this length of sentence; 90 per cent of young males aged 14-16 who are sentenced to custody for less than one year are re-convicted within two years of being released (Ref. 51).

Efficiency and effectiveness

68. Surprisingly, the effectiveness of different kinds of sentence on re-offending by young people is not assessed on a regular basis in most areas of England and Wales, so there is no opportunity to learn from experience. All agencies should help youth justice services to monitor the effectiveness of all disposals given to young people aged 10-17 years on a regular basis, so that they are better placed to advise courts through pre-sentence reports (PSRs) and can provide the magistrates and other agencies on the youth court user group with annual reports on the effects of their sentencing decisions on re-offending.

Exhibit 34
People under 18 sentenced to
immediate custody per 1,000 in the
age group

The use of custodial sentences for 10-17
year olds has fallen in recent years.

Source: Criminal Statistics 1994

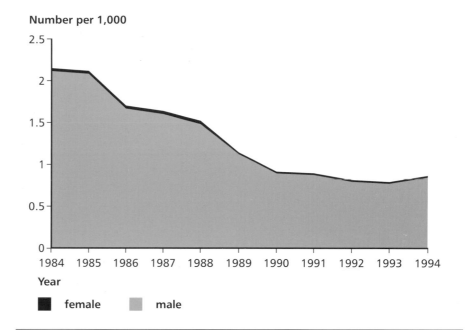

Number per 1,000

Year

■ female   ▨ male

One local authority was able to provide basic information on re-offending, which suggests that it is higher after an attendance centre order than after a supervision order, although the latter is usually given to more serious, or more persistent, offenders (Exhibit 35). Pilot audits by local auditors in other areas give the same result. Since the more severe sentences are generally reserved for the more serious and persistent offenders, previous offending history should be taken into account.

Exhibit 35
Analysis of re-offending rates by
young offenders in Gloucestershire
in one year

Re-offending is higher after an
attendance centre order than after a
supervision order, although the latter is
usually given to more serious, or more
persistent, offenders.

Source: Gloucester Social Services (Ref. 52)

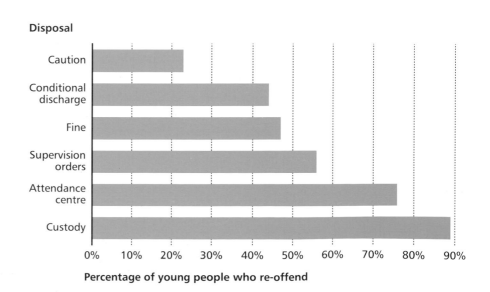

Disposal

Percentage of young people who re-offend

Exhibit 36
Sentencing of 10-17 year olds per
thousand in the age group

Fewer young people are now convicted by
the courts compared with a decade ago and
an increasing proportion of those who are
found guilty are discharged.

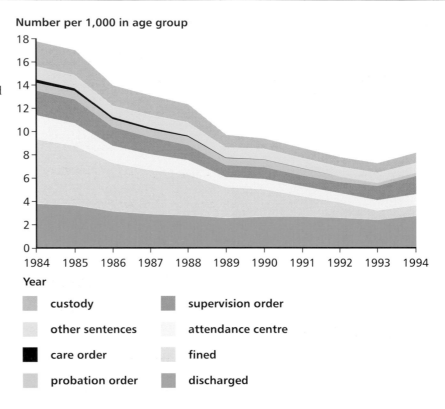

Number per 1,000 in age group

Source: Criminal Statistics 1994

69. Overall, less is done now than a decade ago to address offending by young people. Fewer young people are now convicted by the courts, even allowing for the fall in the number of people aged 10-17 years, and an increasing proportion of those who are found guilty are discharged (Exhibit 36). At 10 of the 12 sites visited, little or no work was done with young offenders outside the court system to address their behaviour.

70. Dealing with young offenders is not cheap. Identifying a young offender costs the police around £1,200. It costs a further £2,500 to prosecute an offender successfully (Exhibit 37). If a young person on remand is placed in local authority secure accommodation, the costs of the court process are further increased.

The criminal justice system and race

71. The criminal justice system must be seen to treat all groups fairly. The main empirical research has been summarised by the Home Office for the Royal Commission on Criminal Justice (Ref. 54). While self-report data suggests that the pattern of offending by white and African Caribbean youths is similar (Ref. 9), African Caribbean youths are more likely than white youths to:

◆ be stopped by the police, though they are no more likely to be arrested as a result than are white youths;

Exhibit 37
Costs of prosecuting a young person

It costs around £1,200 for the police to identify a young offender and a further £2,500 to prosecute an offender successfully.

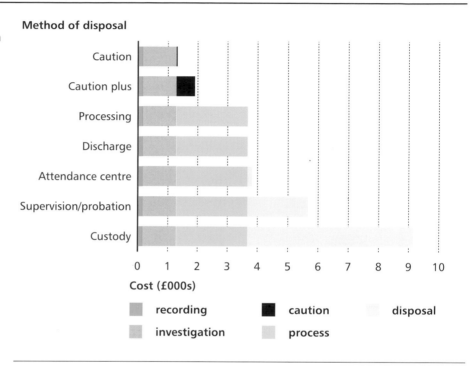

Method of disposal

Cost (£000s)

- recording
- investigation
- caution
- process
- disposal

Source: derived from Milton Keynes Criminal Justice Audit (Ref. 35) and Home Office (Ref. 53)

- be prosecuted rather than cautioned (in part because they are less likely to admit the charges against them);
- be charged with offences which must be heard in the crown court;
- be committed by magistrates to the crown court;
- be remanded in custody;
- plead not guilty;
- be acquitted; and
- receive a custodial sentence.

72. So African Caribbeans are over-represented throughout the system up to and including being acquitted by the court. This pattern suggests that resources may be being used inefficiently by being applied in a discriminatory fashion. Police forces were asked by the Audit Commission in January 1996 how they used the ethnic monitoring information required by the Home Office under Section 95 of the Criminal Justice Act 1991. One-third of forces reported making no use of the data. Other forces reported using it to prepare bi-annual reports for discussion with other agencies and local race equality councils. As from April 1996, all forces are required to monitor local performance on matters such as stop/search, arrest and cautions. Some forces also monitor release without charge and police bail. Regular reports on performance should be discussed with youth justice and other relevant agencies, including community groups. All agencies need to ensure that the criteria they use are not discriminating against minorities and that discretion given to individuals is not used to the disadvantage of minority groups.

A more efficient and effective approach

73. Where a young person admits a first offence, a caution is usually administered and the low rate of re-offending suggests that this is appropriate. For second and third offences, court proceedings may be started but are often dropped. If completed, they often result in a discharge. In many of these cases, the resources consumed in servicing the court could be used more effectively to address offending behaviour directly. One possible model for achieving this is a 'caution plus' action programme, as used by the Northamptonshire Diversion Unit (Box E), which arranges compensation for the victims and addresses the offending behaviour of the young person. The cost of each case is about one-quarter of that of the youth court process. A similar approach has been developed in Holland (Box F), where many young offenders undertake reparation through the HALT scheme, without going to court. A retail theft initiative developed in Milton Keynes invited people arrested for shoplifting to attend meetings to consider the effects of their offence. It gained the support of shopkeepers, reduced re-offending by first time shoplifters and reduced the amount of police time spent processing each offence (Ref. 55).

Box E
The Northamptonshire Diversion Unit

In Northamptonshire the police are likely to warn a young person for a first offence. Those who re-offend once or twice are likely to be referred to the county's Diversion Unit.

- The unit has 29 staff, mainly on secondment from the police, probation, health, social services and the youth service, plus teachers and a few permanent staff, including the director.

- Each referral is allocated to a member of staff who visits the offender to discuss the offence and what reparation the offender would be able and willing to offer.

- The staff member contacts the victim to discuss reparation and whether they wish to meet the offender.

- The staff member produces a draft action plan which covers action to resolve the offence and avoid further offending. These plans are discussed with the team before they are forwarded to the police.

- The police decide whether to administer a caution or recommend prosecution.

Evaluation
- In 1994/95 the unit dealt with 656 young and 570 adult offenders, at a unit cost of £622.

- Seventy-six per cent of the compensation negotiated was paid, with a further 17 per cent being paid in instalments. By comparison, 48 per cent of the compensation ordered by the Inner London Youth Court in 1995/96 was collected.

- The approach appears to reduce re-offending more effectively than most of the formal disposals given by the courts (Exhibit 34). Of the 837 individuals referred to the unit during 1993/94, 35 per cent re-offended after approximately 18 months.

- Seventy-six per cent of victims were satisfied or very satisfied with the resolution of their case, while 10 per cent were dissatisfied.

- Forty per cent of victims whose cases were handled by the unit felt that this approach was more appropriate than going to court, compared with 20 per cent who would have preferred the matter to go to court.

Box F
The HALT scheme

The HALT programme for young offenders was developed in Rotterdam in the 1980s to provide speedier, effective action with young vandals. Petty crime was rising, the criminal justice system took too long to deal with offenders and often ended in no sanction, while cautioning young people was felt to be insufficient. There are now 70 HALT schemes, serving half of Holland's local authorities. Fifty per cent of funding is provided by the Ministry of Justice, with the remainder paid by the local authority.

In the Hague, a police officer can refer an offender under 18 to HALT, provided the cost incurred by the offence is low, and that they admit guilt, are prepared to participate on a voluntary basis and have not already attended twice. A HALT bureau worker writes to the offender and their parents, explaining the choice between HALT and prosecution and inviting them to a meeting. About 85 per cent of young people referred to HALT accept the procedures. The HALT worker then contacts the victim to explore whether, and what sort of, direct reparation might be appropriate. A second conversation with the offender explores the background and reasons for the offending behaviour. HALT then offers a proposal consisting of:

◆ work, relevant to the offence and if possible for the victim;

◆ payment of damages; and/or

◆ an educational component.

Compensation and shaming are important elements. Most Dutch families have public liability insurance which covers the cost of damage by children up to the age of 14. Older children are expected to earn the money to pay compensation themselves. No victim has to meet the offender but, where they do, the offender loses his or her anonymity. Shop staff know why a shoplifter cleaning a shop to atone for a theft is there. Young people cleaning up graffiti wear distinctive, protective clothing, so others know who they are.

In the Hague, one-third of all young offenders are sent to the HALT scheme – around 700 a year. About 95 per cent of programmes are successfully completed; other cases are referred back to the police for prosecution. Forty per cent of HALT participants re-offend, compared with 80 per cent of those who are prosecuted.

74. Local authorities should consider working with the police and courts to develop caution plus schemes, on the lines of the Northamptonshire Diversion Unit and HALT models, for young people who have offended more than once but whose offending is not yet entrenched – to address offending behaviour without processing them through the court. This approach is not suitable for serious or persistent offenders where custody may be at issue, or for cases where guilt is disputed. But many young people going through the youth court are in neither category. If one in five of the young people currently processed through the courts accepted a caution plus programme instead, around £40 million a year could be released to fund services that challenge offending behaviour and prevent crime. To ensure that procedures are followed in a fair and proper manner, substantial action on offending behaviour and compensating victims undertaken outside the court process may need to be overseen, as it is in Northamptonshire, by someone in authority who is not employed by the police force. The official in authority could ensure that young people are not unfairly pressed into admitting guilt and accepting inappropriate interventions. Central government may wish to consider encouraging local services to develop caution plus schemes to reduce re-offending by young people; and how any savings from the more efficient processing of offenders can be released to fund them.

75. The American experience is briefly summarised in Box G. Other countries take a radically different, welfare-based approach to young offenders. The Scottish system is described briefly in Box H. Family conferencing, as developed in New Zealand, is outlined in Box I (p50).

Box G
The American experience

Can we learn from the American experience? Recent falls in recorded crime in the USA are concentrated in a few cities. In New York the police have led a high profile campaign against crime. The programme puts top-down pressure on police commanders and their officers to focus on high-crime spots and make arrests. Considerable effort has been put into getting guns off the street, which has resulted in a fall in the murder rate, and into reducing police corruption. The approach has helped to revitalise a once demoralised force. Other changes in the cities have also helped reduce crime – notably an apparent reduction in the illicit but profitable trade in cocaine. However, the police strategy, and measures of success, do not extend beyond the police role. Police officers do not record all the crime reported to them and there is no victimisation survey in the city. So it is not clear how large the size of the apparent fall in crime in New York has been, or how far police tactics have influenced it.

But the level of crime in the USA remains high compared with other industrialised countries: in 1995 there were more homicides in Los Angeles (849 among a population of 3.5 million) than in England and Wales (746 in a population of 48 million); while 37 of every 100,000 young males aged 15-24 years were killed in 1992 compared to 0.7 per 100,000 in England and Wales. In Philadelphia, between 1987 and 1990, 40 per cent of young males suffered a violent assault serious enough to send them to a hospital emergency room (Ref. 56). The state and federal prison population increased from 196,000 in 1970 to around 1,100,000 in 1996. California, with about half the population of England and Wales, imprisons about three times as many people.

The Federal Government supports preventive work through a Communities that Care programme which helps local communities apply the knowledge that research has provided into factors most likely to encourage positive social attitudes – including supporting and strengthening families, promoting school commitment and success, encouraging responsible sexual behaviour, and promoting safe and cohesive communities. The Rowntree Foundation is considering piloting a United Kingdom version of the programme.

The Children's Hearings System in Scotland deals with most children under 16 without involving the courts. The best interests of the child are always the main consideration. An official – the reporter – oversees the system in each area. A reporter can accept referrals where children are:

- an offender;

- beyond the control of his parent;

- in bad company or exposed to moral danger;

- absent from school regularly without reasonable excuse;

- without parental care, leading to suffering or impaired health or development;

- the victim or potential victim (in the same household) of cruelty or sexual abuse;

- female in a household where incest has been committed;

- referred by a court in England, Wales or Northern Ireland; and

- in the care of the local authority and special measures are needed for care and control.

The reporter can refer the child to social services; deal with the matter themselves – perhaps by warning the child about any poor behaviour and the consequences of poor behaviour in future; or convene a panel hearing. Panel hearings take place in informal settings near to the child's home area. Timed appointments are given and there is not usually much delay in arranging them. Three lay panel members preside, with each panel required to have at least one male and one female member. Normally the child attends, along with their parents and any other relevant individuals such as a social worker or teacher. Parents can be fined if they fail to attend. They, and the child, can choose to take a representative to help them, but legal aid is not available. To help the panel, the recorder can commission reports from any agency: school reports are always required and medical, psychological or psychiatric reports may also be requested. All participants sit round a table and are expected to contribute their views to the discussion. At the end of the discussion, the panel can decide to discharge; request a report from an impartial individual known as a safeguarder; or impose a supervision requirement with or without conditions. Supervision does not last for a fixed period but must be reviewed within a year. If appropriate, it could continue to be renewed until the child is 18 years old. The conditions can include attendance at special projects on offending behaviour or a special education scheme.

For a hearing to take place, the child and parents must accept the grounds for referral stated by the reporter. If the facts are disputed, the case goes to the Sheriff Court for a Proof Hearing, for which legal aid is available. If the child is found guilty, the case is referred back to the panel for a decision. If the child or the parents wish to appeal against the decision of a hearing, this also goes to the sheriff, to be heard within 28 days.

Panel members volunteer from the local community from a wide range of backgrounds and income groups. Members, who are appointed for three to five years, are trained for four to five months in the philosophy of the approach, legislation, the agencies and systems, child development, parenting, local knowledge of community facilities and communication skills. They serve a year of induction before acting as full panel members. Many more people apply to become panel members than are required.

The Recorder's Department in Strathclyde cost £4.4 million in 1994, when 24,000 referrals were received, of which 5,000 were taken to a hearing. So the unit costs were £183 for each referral or £880 for each panel hearing.

Box I
New Zealand: Family Group
Conferences

In New Zealand the 1989 Children and Young People and their Families Act introduced family group conferences as an option for dealing with young offenders. They are based on Maori methods of conflict resolution and can be used as an alternative to court, or as a disposal from court. The key aims are to empower families to make decisions about their children and to exercise authority over them; and to mediate between the victim, or their representative, and the offender. The reintegration of the victim into the family is also seen to be important.

A professional co-ordinator, ethnically matched with the family, arranges for the young person, the family, the victims and the professionals involved to attend a neutral venue, at a time which suits the family and victims – which may be a weekend. The family should include the whole of the extended family, and other individuals important to the young person, such as a sports coach. The young person can bring an advocate with them, often a lawyer. The victims and their supporter, or an advocate for them, are always present.

At the start of the meeting the relevant professionals share their knowledge, views and concerns with the family and answer any questions. They then leave the family to discuss the situation in private and to draw up a plan of action. Any plans have to be carefully recorded and approved by the professionals, but this does not usually prove to be a problem. Most plans involve some kind of reparation, with work, which a family member may arrange. Most take place over a three-month period. Since the focus is strictly on the offending behaviour, welfare issues do not become part of the action plan.

In New Zealand, 50 per cent of victims say that they are satisfied with the outcome (Ref. 57). The satisfaction of the police, the family and the young people has been higher – 91, 85 and 84 per cent respectively. Little evidence is available yet on the impact of conferences on re-offending.

Experience and views of young offenders

76. When young offenders are asked what they think might stop people offending, the most frequent answers are getting a job, and taking part in sport and other leisure activities (Exhibit 38). A number also believe that meeting victims and the threat of prison might deter others from offending.

Exhibit 38
What do young offenders think
would stop others offending?

The most frequent answers are getting a
job, taking part in sport and other leisure
activities.

What would stop others offending?

Jobs 23%
Sport 13%
Other leisure activities 11%
Prison 10%
Meeting victims 10%
Being a victim 9%
Training 9%
More money 5%
Life skills 4%
Other 4%
None 2%

Source: Audit Commission survey of 103 young people on supervision orders

77. The lives of four young offenders, whose offending has been unaffected by the criminal justice system, are outlined in Box J (overleaf) (Ref. 58). Each of these young men has a difficult relationship with his mother and little contact with his father. Parental supervision has been poor, with neither school nor social services managing to fill the gap. Employment prospects do not look encouraging for any of them. Once they began to offend, nothing was done to help them to sort out their lives or to address their offending until they were deeply involved in a criminal way of life. Substantive responses to offending behaviour are expensive and the effects uncertain, so it makes sense to aim to prevent it from developing in the first place. Ways to prevent offending, and other antisocial, behaviour from becoming established in young people are considered in Chapter 2.

Box J
Summary vignettes of four young males whose offending has been unaffected by the criminal justice system

	family	school	peer group	training and work	drugs and alcohol	known offending history		
						age	offence	action
Billy	Eldest of four children; father in prison; mother unemployed. Billy missing from home for long periods when five years old.	Poor achiever; truanted persistently until excluded at age 14.	Offends with others; 17 known associates.	Declines YT as offending more lucrative. No benefits.		8	criminal damage	none
						10	shop theft	caution
						11	theft	caution
						11	handling	caution
						12	theft	fine
						13	burglary	conditional discharge
						16	burglary	supervision order
						16	theft, burglary, handling	supervision order
						16	theft from car, etc	coming up in court
Terry	Father in prison; Terry's relationship with mother fraught; left on own for long periods aged 12.	Truanted for most of 18-month period up to age 15, when excluded.	Has around 20 friends, who spend a lot of time at his mother's house causing her distress.	No interest in training or work. Sees father's career as professional criminal as a model of how to earn money.	Heavy cannabis user.	8	burglary	none
						9	shop theft	none
						11	commercial burglary	caution
						13	shop theft	caution
						14	theft from cars	conditional discharge
						14	burglary, theft	attendance centre order
						16	eight offences	supervision order
						16	two offences	supervision order with specified activities
						17	six offences	custody for four months
						17	further offences	attendance centre order
Keith	Parents separated when Keith aged two; moved between them until grandparents took him in; became homeless aged 16 when they refused to put up with his absences and late night reappearances.	Attendance sporadic; gave up attending aged 15.	17 known associates.	Started engineering job on Saturday mornings aged 14. Lost job aged 16.	Drinks heavily.	14	carried in stolen car	caution
						15	taking cars	caution
						15	taking cars	caution
						15	interfering with vehicle	conditional discharge
						16	burglary	probation order
						16	theft from car	supervision order
						16	breached supervision order	combination order
Phil	Parents separated when Phil aged four; lives with mother with whom he has stormy relationship; mother has a history of being abused by men. Into voluntary care aged 10 but absconded back to mother, who wanted him back but could not cope. Attacked mother with knife, causing her to seek hospital treatment.	Excluded from junior school; re-admitted but became permanent truant; education ceased at 13 when in care - moving continually between residential care and home.		Has worked in scrapyard for cash in hand. Wants to be seen as worker but has poor prospects.		8	stealing a car and arson	none
						10	theft	caution
						11	theft	caution
						11	theft	caution
						15	stealing cars	attendance centre order
						15	burglary, car offences	supervision order
						16	burglary	supervision order
						17	aggravated burglary	unresolved

Conclusions

78. The current system for dealing with young offenders could be improved in a number of ways, set out below. Local audit work by the Commission's auditors will focus on local authority youth justice services in 1997 and again in 1998. The local audits will cover the number of days it takes to process cases from arrest to sentence; the use made of youth justice service workers' time; the use made of caution plus schemes; and the rates of offending before and after different sentences and cautioning packages. Audit reports will include comparative information showing performance in different parts of England and Wales.

Recommendations

Action for all agencies

1   Youth court user groups for all agencies involved in the youth court, including youth justice services, should meet regularly; and agree local targets for the average number of days it takes, from arrest, before a young person is sentenced by the youth court.

2   Persistent offenders should receive more intensive supervision in the community, with programmes that draw on the research about which approaches work.

3   All agencies should help youth justice services to monitor the effects of all disposals given to young people aged 10-17 years on a regular basis, so that they are better placed to advise courts through PSRs and can provide the magistrates and other agencies on the youth court user group with annual reports on the effects of their sentencing decisions on re-offending.

4   All agencies need to ensure that the criteria they use are not discriminating against minorities and that discretion given to individuals is not used to the disadvantage of minority groups.

5   Local authorities should consider working with the police and courts to develop caution plus schemes – on the lines of the Northamptonshire Diversion Unit and HALT models, for young people who have offended more than once but whose offending is not yet entrenched – to address offending behaviour without processing them through the court.

Action for social services, with others

6   Social services departments that do not use volunteers to fulfil the appropriate adult role should consider doing so, to free around 10 per cent of the time of youth justice workers (equivalent to around £2 million). Around half of this saving will be needed to recruit, train and co-ordinate the volunteers.

7   Social services should ensure that they have suitable accommodation for young people transferred to them by the police until they can appear in court. Guidance to social workers on what to do if the young person starts to leave the accommodation should be agreed with the police.

8 Social services should consider, with the local probation service, whether to form joint youth justice service teams.

9 Social services departments that do not provide a bail support service should consider doing so.

10 Local authority secure units should be able to identify their costs and charge fees sufficient to cover them.

11 Staff involved in the preparation of PSRs should have the appropriate skills and knowledge and receive appropriate training and supervision.

12 Youth justice services should canvass magistrates' views on the value of the PSRs that they provide each year – more often if the magistrates wish.

13 Youth justice services and probation could usefully consider how the knowledge and expertise of psychologists, among other disciplines, can be used to help devise, implement and monitor behavioural and cognitive-behavioural programmes in community settings.

14 Youth justice services and probation should ensure that good use is made of publicly funded facilities that are intended to address offending behaviour by young people, by discussing with magistrates the sort of young people who would benefit from them.

15 Youth justice services should consider using mentoring schemes for those on supervision orders, to give the young offender support and encouragement in addressing their behaviour.

Action for the police, with others

16 Police forces that have not already done so could usefully discuss and agree gravity factors with social services, to improve consistency of decision-making and reduce the amount of interagency discussion of individual cases.

17 All police forces should consider whether they could use existing resources more effectively by having youth and community sections in order to liaise with other public services dealing with young people, notably the CPS, social services and local education authorities.

18 Police forces should consider giving officers who caution young offenders training in how to do so.

19 Police forces could make more effective use of their officers' time by simplifying the internal paperwork required for dealing with young people. Interview summaries forwarded to the CPS should be kept brief, with a copy of the relevant tape made available if more information is needed by the CPS or defence lawyers.

20 Police forces should ensure that offenders are cautioned where guilt is admitted but cases have been discontinued.

Action for the youth courts

21 Youth courts should consider piloting pre-trial reviews, to establish their effectiveness in reducing the time wasted by people who attend trials that do not take place.

Action for the CPS

22 The CPS could help to expedite cases through the youth court by passing papers needed to prepare PSRs directly to the service preparing the report.

Action for central government

23 Central government may wish to consider encouraging local services to develop caution plus schemes to address offending by young people; and how any savings from the more efficient processing of offenders can be released to fund local services that succeed in reducing offending by young people through caution plus schemes.

Offending by young people is associated with a range of risk factors including inadequate parental supervision; aggressive or hyperactive behaviour in early childhood; truancy and exclusion from school; peer group pressure to offend; unstable living conditions; lack of training and employment; and drug and alcohol abuse.

These factors can be used to help target measures to prevent crime by identifying areas where young people are at risk. Schemes to address the factors need to be piloted and evaluated in high-risk areas.

2 Preventing Youth Crime

Introduction

79. While public services clearly need to deal effectively with offending behaviour by young people, it would be better to prevent the offending behaviour in the first place. Appropriate help and support for young people who are at risk of offending, but have not yet done so, can prevent some of them from getting involved in crime. Although there is no way of predicting accurately which individuals are going to offend, young people in certain categories or circumstances are at much greater risk than others. The factors associated with a high risk of offending have been comprehensively described by Farrington (Ref. 59). They include gender, with boys more likely to offend than girls; inadequate parenting; aggressive and hyperactive behaviour in early childhood; truancy and exclusion from school; peer group pressure to offend; unstable living conditions; lack of training and employment; and drug and alcohol abuse. Those who experience many or all of these factors throughout their childhood and teenage years are at the highest risk of getting caught up in a cycle of antisocial behaviour, including offending, which is then difficult to break (Exhibit 39). Those who start offending at an early age are more likely to become persistent offenders (Ref. 60).

Exhibit 39
Cycle of antisocial behaviour

Young people can get caught up in a cycle of antisocial behaviour which is difficult to break.

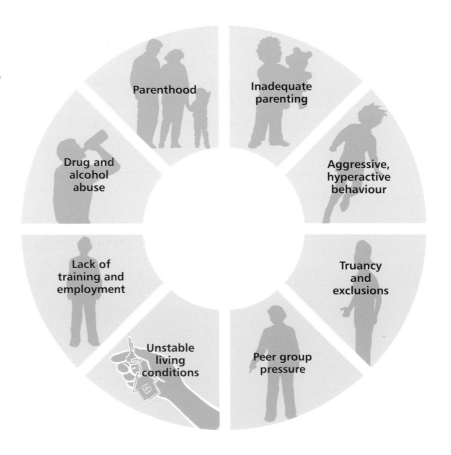

Source: Audit Commission

'Steps can be taken by a wide range of agencies, to address problems before those at risk start to offend.'

80. These factors can be used to help target measures to prevent crime, by identifying areas where young people are at high risk. Steps can be taken by a wide range of agencies, to address problems before those at risk start to offend. Those responsible include:

- parents, who can be helped to bring children up to respect the law and the rights of other people;
- schools, which play a key role – although they, in turn, require help if they are to contain and deal effectively with the problems that difficult children present;
- social services;
- health;
- leisure services and the youth service;
- housing;
- training agencies; and
- drug and alcohol services.

81. Few programmes for preventing offending by young people in England and Wales have been thoroughly evaluated. Some of the crime prevention programmes for pre-school children in other countries have been evaluated, and have demonstrated their effectiveness convincingly. But programmes for young children take a long time to have an effect. Interventions with older children also need to be evaluated, by establishing:

- the number of children or young people affected by a particular risk factor;
- the proportion who go on to offend;
- options for addressing the risk factor;
- the cost of these options;
- the reduction in offending behaviour that results; and
- benefits, in terms of lower crime and any other significant positive outcomes.

82. Much of this information is absent or incomplete. In part, this reflects poor co-ordination between the different agencies dealing with young people, often with different objectives; and in part it results from the low priority given to evaluating public spending by some of the agencies concerned. Problems vary from community to community. So must solutions. But learning from the experience of others can be useful, and the options identified below have been shown to have a positive effect on the behaviour of young people. Without sound evaluation, it is impossible to judge whether investing in such options saves money overall – so all schemes should be properly costed and monitored. Pilot studies should be targeted on the areas of greatest need, which suffer most crime and are home to many young offenders.

Family factors

83. Research has shown that children who are brought up in families with lax parental supervision and in poor neighbourhoods have a higher risk of becoming offenders (Ref. 61). A growing proportion of children are experiencing these factors. The percentage of children living in households with less than half of the average national income, after housing costs, rose from 16 to 33 per cent between 1981 and 1992. Inequality of income (as measured by the Gini coefficient, a commonly used index) is greater in the UK than in other Northern European countries (Ref. 62). Bringing up children in poverty is difficult. For a couple with three children, half of the average income after housing costs amounted to £11,000 in 1994/95. This contrasts with an estimated average £4,000 a year spent by families to care for one child up to the age of five (Ref. 63). In most two-parent families, either both parents are in employment or neither parent is; either way, family life can be difficult. Where both parents work, there may be little time to look after the children. Where neither parent works, the need to cope on very little money often puts extra stress on family relationships (Ref. 64). It can be particularly difficult for those in lone-parent families – and the percentage of children brought up in such families rose from 11 to 19 per cent between 1981 and 1992 (Exhibit 40).

84. Neighbourhoods where large numbers of young offenders live are more deprived, as measured by the DoE Index of Local Conditions: in the West Midlands the correlation is 0.3 per cent (Exhibit 41). The same correlation exists between deprivation and reports of juvenile disturbances in Merseyside (Ref. 65). Targeting resources on deprived neighbourhoods would help address

Exhibit 40
Children living in lone-parent families

The percentage of children brought up in lone-parent families rose from 11 to 19 per cent between 1981 and 1992.

Note:
UK. The figures exclude children living with unmarried couples.

Source: Office of Population Censuses and Surveys

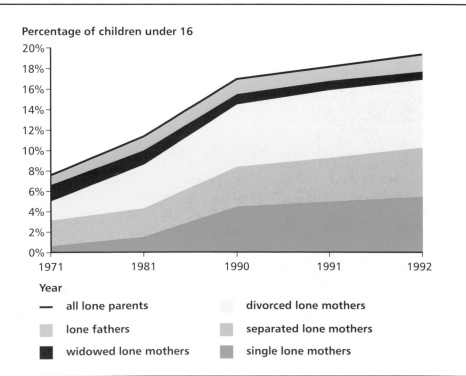

Percentage of children under 16

Exhibit 41
Social deprivation and young offenders

Neighbourhoods where large numbers of young offenders live are more deprived, as measured by the DoE Index of Local Conditions: the correlation is 0.3 per cent in the West Midlands.

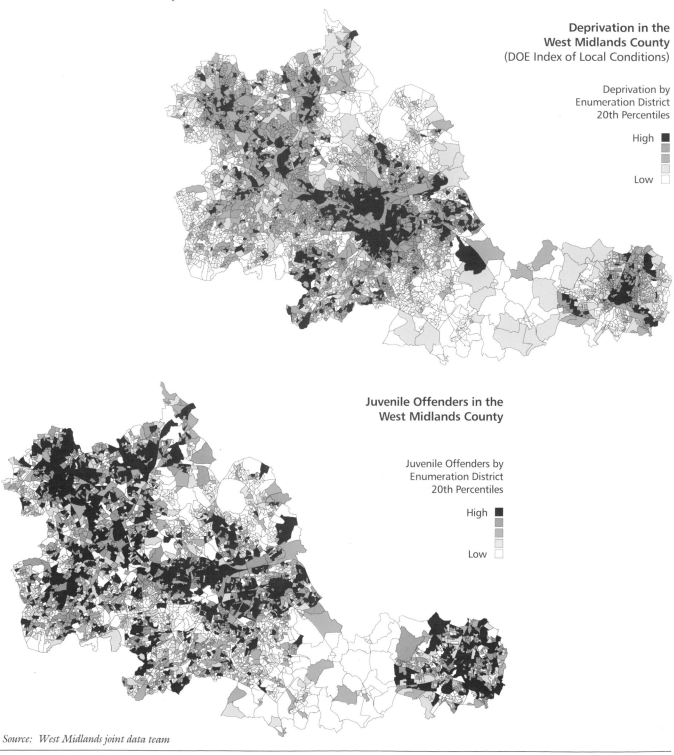

**Deprivation in the
West Midlands County**
(DOE Index of Local Conditions)

Deprivation by
Enumeration District
20th Percentiles

High

Low

**Juvenile Offenders in the
West Midlands County**

Juvenile Offenders by
Enumeration District
20th Percentiles

High

Low

Source: West Midlands joint data team

factors associated with offending by young people, without rewarding criminal behaviour.

85. While it is useful to be able to predict the local areas in which children are most likely to become delinquent – on the basis of family size, social status and parental separation – these factors are also able to identify three-quarters of individual offenders but they over-predict fivefold (Ref. 66). Predicting the future behaviour of individuals is more closely linked to factors such as parental conflict and the quality of family life in the early years, although these are more difficult to measure.

86. Inadequate parenting is strongly associated with later offending. Neglect by parents, poor maternal and domestic care before the age of five years, insecure attachment, family conflict and the absence of a good relationship with either parent have all been shown to increase the risk of behaviour problems and subsequent offending (Refs. 67, 68, 69). Young people who say that their attachment to their family is weak are more likely to report that they have committed offences (Ref. 9), as are those who have experienced cruelty and abuse at the hands of parents (Ref. 70). The nature of parental supervision is also important. Parents who rely heavily on harsh punishment, or who are erratic in their discipline, are twice as likely to have children who offend (Ref. 71). Harsh punishment is also associated with more violent and more frequent offending (Ref. 72).

87. If family members engage in crime, children are likely to copy their behaviour (Ref. 73). Parental conflict experienced by children when they are young is also associated with later offending (Refs. 74, 75). The children of step families are also more likely to offend later on (Ref. 76). In lone-parent families, the absence of a male authority figure in the lives of young children – either at home or school – may have an adverse effect on their behaviour (Ref. 77).

Improving parenting

88. Parents, even those with difficulties, are very important to their children. Most young offenders on supervision orders who were interviewed by the Audit Commission said that parents were the most important influence on their lives (Exhibit 42). A Home Office study (Ref. 9) has shown that 21 per cent of young people aged 14-25 had a weak attachment to their family and nearly half (47 per cent) went on to offend, compared with only 29 per cent of those with a strong attachment. Over half (56 per cent) received a low or medium level of supervision from their parents, of whom 42 per cent went on to offend, compared with only 20 per cent of those who received a high level of supervision. So improving family relationships and parental supervision of poorly supervised children could potentially reduce their offending significantly.

' Parents who rely heavily on harsh punishment, or who are erratic in their discipline, are twice as likely to have children who offend. Harsh punishment is also associated with more violent and more frequent offending.'

Exhibit 42
Those who are important to young
offenders

Most young offenders interviewed said
that parents were the most important
influence on their lives.

People who are important

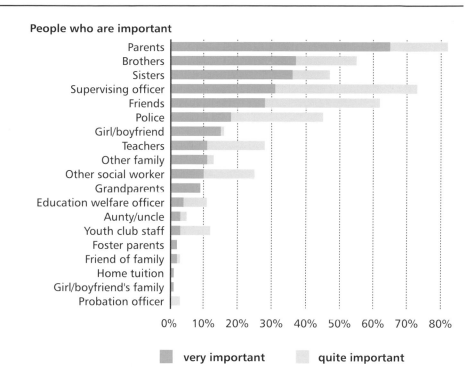

*Source: Audit Commission survey of 103 young
people on supervision orders*

89. Parents who are bringing up their children in difficult circumstances can be helped by professionals (or by volunteer, experienced parents) to improve their parenting skills and produce better behaved, more trustworthy children who need less expensive supervision and intervention later on (Ref. 78). Parent education aims to help parents develop self-awareness and self-confidence and improve their capacity to support and nurture their children (Ref. 64). An American study, in which family members were trained to negotiate effectively, stick to clear rules and to reward good behaviour, led to a halving of offending rates (Ref. 79). A family support programme in Yale provided structured home visits and day-care to low-income, lone parents for their children's first two or three years. Ten years later, the parents were more involved in their children's schools and had also gained more educational qualifications themselves (Ref. 80).

90. Family centres, which may bring together staff from social services, health services and voluntary organisations, can be a good way to assist whole families and to promote networks of parents for mutual support. One large multi-agency centre in the Midlands serves approximately 300 parents per day, who use either the nursery, a drop-in centre, various groups or other facilities, at a total cost of roughly £600,000 per annum. Homestart, a voluntary organisation, facilitates the befriending of young families who may be at risk, using volunteer networks of experienced parents in over 150 local schemes. Eighty per cent of the families befriended have reported improvements in their ability to cope, and health visitors' ratings tend to concur with this (Ref. 81). Newpin, which developed from Homestart, helps depressed mothers by

providing local support networks for up to a year. Some 17 centres have been developed in the UK. No detailed evaluation has yet been carried out, but mothers report improvements in their mental state and feelings of control over their own lives. The Oxford Family Nurturing Project – described in the Audit Commission report, *Seen But Not Heard* (Ref. 82) – is another good example of support and guidance for parents, which is provided by a voluntary organisation working closely with local health and social services professionals. The project provides 15-week programmes for 50 families a year, at a cost of £85,000. Evaluation of the effects of these schemes on the children's behaviour is badly needed.

91. Despite the preventive philosophy built into the Children Act 1989, social services departments have found it difficult to move from a reactive social policing role, which focuses on child protection cases, towards more proactive work that supports families (Ref. 82). The Department of Health is currently considering how to move towards a broader approach to meeting the needs of children and families, such as jointly funded family centres, and thereby reduce the need for crisis work in child protection (Ref. 83).

92. In conjunction with education, health visitors and mental health services, social services should consider piloting schemes in deprived areas to provide guidance on parenting and assistance to those with difficulties through family centres and volunteer programmes. Their effects on the children's behaviour should be evaluated. Promising options include: multi-agency family centres – which may include social workers, health visitors or volunteer projects – in deprived neighbourhoods; and volunteer programmes that link new parents living in high risk areas with experienced parents who are able to offer practical help and support for an hour or two a week – along the lines of the Homestart and Newpin programmes. In high-risk areas that do not have family centres, social services and health services should consider piloting such programmes. In other cases, reference to guidance on parenting may be appropriate – for example, *Toddler Taming* (Ref. 84), and *Families and How to Survive Them* (Ref. 85).

Early childhood behaviour

93. It may be possible to identify children early on who could benefit from targeted help and thereby avoid problems later on. Characteristics such as low birthweight and having problems shortly after birth; poor performance in IQ tests at age three; and early childhood behaviour which is aggressive, hyperactive, impulsive or disruptive (Refs. 86, 87, 88) are key identifiers. Health visitors are likely to have a key role in identifying the local areas and families which may be most at risk.

94. Specific parent-training programmes currently being evaluated by some child and adolescent mental health services (CAMHS) could help many young children with behaviour problems. School-age children can be taught to solve problems in structured ways and their parents given separate training. One successful approach provided children with 25 treatment sessions of 50 minutes over six to eight months and the parents 16 sessions of 1.5 hours. At the end of the treatment, and a year later, more than half of a group of 97 children with significant behaviour problems were rated by both parents and teachers as

' Local education authorities should consider targeting schemes to provide intensive, structured pre-school education to areas of high risk and deprivation.'

behaving within the normal range, although the persistence of these positive effects throughout childhood has yet to be confirmed. Involving parents is important, but difficult to achieve with those at greatest risk because they are most likely to fail to complete the course (Ref. 89).

95. However, the level and type of child and adolescent mental health service in England and Wales varies widely. A survey of English districts found that the number of consultant psychiatrists ranged from 15.6 to 0.4 per 100,000 children. The number of specialist staff provided was unrelated to need, as indicated by the Jarman Index of deprivation (Ref. 90). The staffing mix also varied; one-third of the 151 CAMHS in the survey were without nurses, almost one-third without clinical psychologists, one-fifth without social workers and one had no psychiatrist. Child and adolescent mental health services should ensure that they have expertise in dealing with conduct disorders. The Health Advisory Service, in its 1995 review of children at risk services, emphasised the importance of primary level work in settings such as family centres. Mental health professionals should place greater priority on indirect work, supporting health visitors, family centres and voluntary groups that deal with children whose behaviour is difficult – and should monitor the effects of this work. As part of their commissioning process, health commissioning authorities should specify support to these groups in their contracts with mental health providers, and monitoring and evaluation.

Structured nursery education with home support

96. Early childhood behaviour which is aggressive or disruptive can be addressed by intensive, structured nursery education, targeted to those at risk. The best known example is the High/Scope project in Michigan, USA (Ref. 91). In this programme, a sample of young children who received pre-school education and parental support was compared with a matched sample which did not. The education was carefully structured so the children could choose and plan their educational activities, carry them out in a systematic way and review what they had achieved. Some experts believe that more highly structured approaches may be preferable for children who are mentally ill-equipped to make such decisions and carry them out successfully. Nevertheless, important features of the programme included a high level of support: the ratio of teachers to pupils was kept at or below ten to one; and the parents were encouraged to become closely involved, through weekly home visits and invitations to classroom sessions. An evaluation over 23 years found that children who had been on the programme caused less criminal damage, incurred lower costs to the criminal justice system, paid more tax and required less remedial schooling. They were also more likely to stay in school and gain qualifications; and more were employed and in better jobs. The benefits were worth $7 for every $1 spent. Local education authorities should consider targeting schemes to provide intensive, structured pre-school education and home support for three and four year olds, in which parents are involved, to areas of high risk and deprivation; and they should be evaluated. Providers of pre-school education should consider helping parents to reinforce the discipline that they teach.

Problems at school

97. Where parents fail to socialise their children adequately, schools have to cope with bad behaviour among their pupils. When this occurs at an early age, offending is more likely to develop later on (Ref. 92). Poor school performance is also a good predictor of later delinquency (Ref. 74). So it is worrying that an increasing number of pupils are being excluded from school.

98. Permanent exclusions have risen threefold since 1990/91 (Exhibit 43). The figures published for 1990/91 and 1991/92 probably understate the true totals, but there has been a substantial increase in recent years. More than half of the authorities visited also admitted that 'informal' or 'backdoor' exclusions took place, and that the frequency of these was also increasing. In such cases, the school advises parents to withdraw their child from a particular school and look for a place elsewhere. One local authority found that 58 per cent of those children aged 11 or over who had been permanently excluded offended either in the year before or the year after their exclusion. The group was known to commit 50 per cent more offences in the year following exclusion than in the previous year (Ref. 93).

99. Young people who truant or are excluded from school are more likely to offend (Exhibit 44). Exclusion and truancy are therefore both key indicators of trouble to come, if corrective action is not taken. Forty-two per cent of offenders of school age who are sentenced in the youth court have been excluded from school (Exhibit 45). A further 23 per cent truant significantly. Twenty per cent have a statement of special education needs (compared with 2-3 per cent of all secondary school children) but few receive substantial help with those needs once they are outside school.

Exhibit 43
Pupils excluded from school

Permanent exclusions have risen threefold since 1990/91.

Source: DfEE

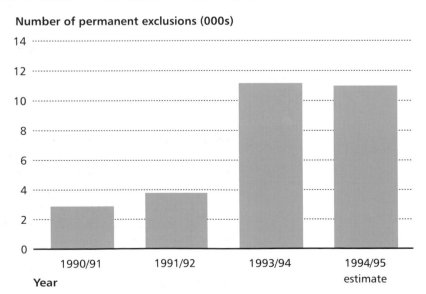

Number of permanent exclusions (000s)

Year

Exhibit 44
School factors and offending

Young people who truant or are excluded from school are more likely to offend.

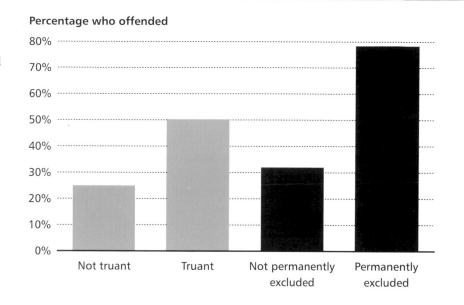

Percentage who offended

Source: Graham and Bowling (Ref. 9)

Exhibit 45
Young offenders' (of school age) absence from school

Sixty-five per cent of young offenders of school age who are sentenced in court have been excluded from school or truant significantly.

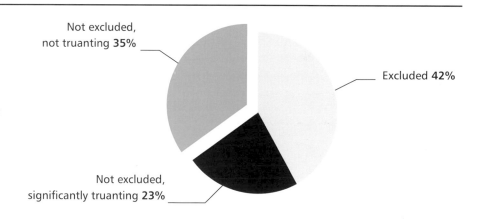

Not excluded, not truanting **35%**

Excluded **42%**

Not excluded, significantly truanting **23%**

Source: Audit Commission survey of 600 young offenders sentenced in court

100. The rate of exclusion varies considerably between different schools, even where the catchment populations are similar (Ref. 94) but, in general, schools in areas of higher social deprivation are more likely to exclude pupils (Ref. 95). Boys are more often excluded than girls. And students of African Caribbean origin are more likely to be excluded than others; between 1990 and 1992 African Caribbean students accounted for 2 per cent of the school-age population but over 8 per cent of permanent exclusions (Ref. 96).

101. The antipathy between school and the disruptive child is usually mutual, and disaffected young people who are not excluded often truant from school. Truancy is much more widespread than exclusion; a survey of pupils in years 10 and 11 of school found that one in ten pupils missed school at least once a week (Ref. 97). The true figures may be higher still, as many of the most frequent truants would have been absent on the day of the survey. Figures published by the DfEE for 1994/95 show that secondary school children missed an average of 9.2 per cent of school registrations (including authorised absences) at the start of morning and afternoon sessions (Ref. 98). Actual absence levels are higher, as many truants leave school after registration.

102. Truancy rates vary widely between individual schools. In some, almost one-quarter of the half-day sessions are missed. The same schools also tend to achieve lower exam passes (Exhibit 46). Pupils with behavioural problems often have unrecognised difficulties in learning, so are unlikely to be able to achieve many of the academic standards valued by school league tables. Action to address truancy needs to be targeted on the schools with the greatest problems and the local areas that they serve.

103. Truants generally go home or to friends' homes, to do 'nothing in particular'. Others spend much of the day in bed, and stay out until the early hours of the morning (Ref. 99), when they tend to mix with older peers and their parents have little control over their way of life.

School support

104. Schools provide opportunities for both academic and social education, through adult role models and peer group relationships. The way that schools are run can make a great deal of difference to pupils' behaviour in and out of class, including offending, their attendance, and their academic achievements.

Exhibit 46
School absences and GCSE passes by 11-16 year olds in one county

Schools with high truancy rates tend to achieve lower exam passes.

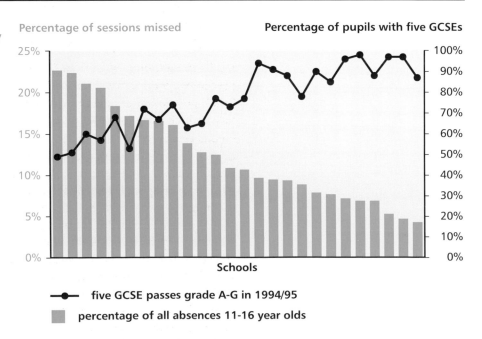

Percentage of sessions missed

Percentage of pupils with five GCSEs

Schools

● five GCSE passes grade A-G in 1994/95

percentage of all absences 11-16 year olds

Sources: CIPFA, DfEE

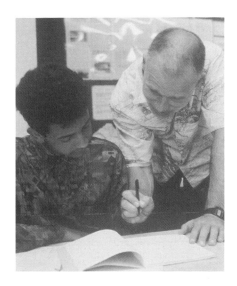

Successful schools have:

♦ high expectations for both work and behaviour;

♦ clear disciplinary rules, especially positive encouragement and sparing use of punishment;

♦ models of good behaviour from teachers;

♦ good teacher-child relationships;

♦ respect for the children and their achievements;

♦ opportunities for children and their parents to be involved in the organisation of the school;

♦ pleasant physical conditions; and

♦ a supportive and coherent structure for teachers (Ref. 100).

Schools, with the help of support services, should reinforce good behaviour, encouraging the involvement of parents.

105. Classroom interventions can improve children's academic and recreational activities, social skills and management by teachers and parents. For example, programmes called the Good Behaviour Game and Mastery Learning have been shown to reduce aggressive and disruptive behaviour in the classroom (Ref. 101). These have led children to improve their academic performance and self-esteem over three years. Strategies to reduce bullying in schools are important in helping pupils to learn appropriate behaviour and to deal authoritatively with those who behave in antisocial ways. Pupils should be encouraged to report incidents of bullying and supported when they do so. Supervision of playground areas is also important.

106. Local education authorities (LEAs) provide support through school psychology services for teachers dealing with disruptive children. Mental health professionals, such as psychologists and psychiatric nurses, could also help. The Health Advisory Service, in its 1995 review of child and adolescent mental health services (Ref. 102), emphasised the importance of primary level mental health work of this kind in settings such as schools. At the sites visited, the school psychology services were largely used to assess or support statements of special educational need – of which only about one in five were for children with emotional or behavioural problems. Mental health professionals interviewed – who said they had provided support to schools in the past – reported that health commissioners were no longer prepared to fund activity to help teachers deal with difficult pupils. Child mental health services should offer support to teachers in schools dealing with pupils with behaviour problems, particularly those in high-risk areas. Health commissioners need to ensure that contracts with healthcare providers specify pilot programmes designed to advise and assist schools dealing with pupils with behavioural problems in areas of high risk and deprivation, and evaluate their effects.

Reducing truancy and exclusion

107. Reducing the number of pupils who are not at school for reasons of truancy or exclusion could significantly reduce the number of young offenders in a local area. Half of truants offend, but only one-quarter of non-truants do (Exhibit 43). If half of the truants returned to school, and the returned truants were as likely to offend as the non-truants, the percentage of offenders in the age group could be reduced from 35 to 30 per cent. Similarly, three-quarters of excluded pupils offend, but only one-third of those who are not excluded. This group contains some of the more persistent offenders (Audit Commission evidence from 600 offenders), so tackling truancy and exclusions, involving pupils' families, is one way to provide targeted assistance to a group who are at high risk of offending.

108. Parents are responsible for ensuring that their children get a full-time education. If they do not, LEAs are responsible for taking action, although they are under pressure to delegate the resources for doing so to schools. Moreover, there is no agreement on how to tackle truancy. Within the LEA, education welfare officers have the main responsibility. But fewer than one-quarter have a professional training (Ref. 103), usually a general social work qualification; there is no agreement on how they should tackle their job and little central monitoring of what they are doing. In practice, the service operates very differently in different authorities. In some, officers leave the main action to teachers and deal only with individuals and families referred to them by schools, on a casework and counselling basis. Others run programmes that target particular schools or neighbourhoods intensively for brief periods. Some resort to legal action against parents, under the 1993 Education Act, for not ensuring that their child had a full-time education. A survey of 55 LEAs showed that in 1993/94, out of 2,000 parents summonsed, 70 per cent were fined (the average fine varying from £40 in one area to £240 in another); 25 per cent were found not guilty or discharged; and 5 per cent were redirected for an educational supervision order, which requires that a social worker befriend, assist and give direction to children and their parents (Ref. 103).

109. Successful approaches to truancy and disruptive behaviour often involve parents, who may condone absence from school. Any emotional and behavioural difficulties need to be identified at an early stage, as emphasised by guidance from the Department of Education and Employment (DfEE) and Welsh Office. The Truancy and Disaffected Pupils programme of the DfEE has been providing support for programmes to combat truancy and pupil disaffection, and has cost approximately £14 million a year over four years. An equivalent programme in Wales provides £920,000 a year. The evaluation commissioned by DfEE found that the interventions which best improved attendance and reduced disaffection were:

◆ preventive work by teachers and support staff in primary schools and in the early years of secondary schools to prevent later, hard-core absenteeism;

' Successful approaches to truancy and disruptive behaviour often involve parents, who may condone absence from school.'

'Exclusion and assessment for a statement of special educational needs are usually considered by different people and procedures within schools and LEAs.'

- contact with the home of an absent pupil on the first day of absence; and
- the opportunity for all pupils and staff in the school community to be involved in developing a policy on attendance.

Those carrying out the evaluation were unable to assess the impact of these schemes on local offending by young people, as most police forces said that they did not have the resources to collect and analyse the information (Ref. 104).

110. Some schools with above-average truancy rates develop strategies for reducing them, drawing on good practices such as those developed and promoted by DfEE under one of the Grants for Education Support and Training (GEST) programmes – which encourage schools and LEAs to tackle truancy. For example, a scheme in Newcastle releases teachers for one day per week to undertake home visits, accompany parents to meetings or to run workshops for parents to help them to deal with difficult behaviour in their children. Some parents who were previously difficult to engage are getting more involved; many are gaining confidence in managing their children's behaviour. However, there is no effective regional or national network through which good practice can be shared. Dissemination of good practice within LEAs, where this occurs, is much valued by schools. LEAs should, as part of their community safety strategy, consider encouraging schools to develop strategies for addressing truancy where absenteeism is high, drawing on good practice promoted by the DfEE, and monitoring their effects. The police and other local services should help evaluate the impact of such schemes on juvenile nuisance and offending by young people. Social services could pilot the attachment of family support workers to schools in deprived areas, to help keep young people at risk in school.

111. In some areas, exclusions are avoided through schools, LEAs or social services making support available, including support teachers and counselling. The Peers school in Oxford, which serves an area of high social deprivation, has a special needs unit, a team of support teachers and a counsellor. Pupils with behavioural problems are taught for part of the time in the special unit and, for the remainder, in the classroom with support teachers. Counselling is available for pupils with problems of any kind and their families. The ethos of the school encourages shared responsibility and high standards of behaviour from both pupils and staff.

112. Exclusion and assessment for a statement of special educational needs are usually considered by different people and procedures within schools and LEAs. A pupil with emotional and behavioural problems could be referred either to the special education needs co-ordinator for an assessment of special educational needs, or to the head of discipline to begin the process of exclusion. Assessment of special needs is more difficult after exclusion unless and until the child is admitted to another school. All exclusion decisions have to be approved by an exclusions panel, which consists of LEA representatives in directly managed schools and the governors in grant-maintained schools. Two local authorities visited linked the process for considering the special education needs of pupils – which include emotional and behavioural

difficulties – with the process for excluding children, by asking schools whether they had considered any special educational needs of each pupil before exclusion. The DfEE Circular 10/94 recommends that exclusion should occur only if:

◆ the school has taken all reasonable steps to avoid excluding the child; and

◆ allowing the child to remain in school would be seriously detrimental to the education or welfare of the pupil, or to that of others at the school.

Where pupils are excluded, LEAs should require schools to confirm that their special educational needs have been fully considered.

113. Helping pupils who have been excluded from school can be difficult. The pupils themselves are almost always anxious to return to school, regardless of age or the reason for exclusion (Ref. 105). An LEA can direct another school to accept an excluded pupil, provided that there is a spare place. But many schools are full, so the pupil may have to travel some distance. Even when schools have spare places, they can be reluctant to take a disruptive pupil; one of the LEAs visited had twice had to ask the Secretary of State to direct a particular school to accept an excluded pupil. Nationally, only 15 per cent of pupils excluded from secondary schools return to a mainstream school (Ref. 106). LEAs should promote the re-integration of excluded children into school.

114. LEAs are required to offer some educational provision for pupils who are permanently excluded if their parents have been unable to find a place for them in another school. This can amount to as little as four hours of home tuition per week, or one or two hours per day in a special Pupil Referral Unit. Consequently, these children spend most of their waking hours with nothing in particular to do, and have few positive goals to work towards.

115. Another authority visited commissioned an independent agency, Cities in Schools, to help re-integrate pupils into mainstream schools (Box K). Social services departments should consider piloting schemes in which family support workers are attached to schools in deprived areas, to address truancy and behaviour problems at an early stage. LEAs should consider commissioning independent agencies, such as Cities in Schools, in areas with particular problems, to help disaffected pupils return to school, and to provide effective alternatives for pupils out of school.

' Even when schools have spare places, they can be reluctant to take a disruptive pupil; one of the LEAs visited had twice had to ask the Secretary of State to direct a particular school to accept an excluded pupil.'

Cities in Schools works with young people with school attendance and behavioural problems, including non-attendance and exclusion. It aims to address the underlying problems, rebuild self-esteem and re-integrate these young people into mainstream education and training, so that they can fulfil their potential. In South Glamorgan, Cities in Schools provides four programmes, ranging from intensive individual intervention to preventive services.

- Two **bridge courses for year 11**: a personal tutor is given the resources to organise a weekly programme for ten pupils not attending school to attend for two days at a local further education college, two days work-related experience and one day in tutorial and structured leisure time. The personal tutor liaises with the family, care provider and other agencies and becomes a mentor to give new direction to these pupils' lives. The aims include helping young people to improve their literacy, numeracy and life skills, to develop constructive leisure interests and explore career options; and helping social workers provide positive alternatives to care and custody. Pupils' progress is reviewed after every 12 weeks (cost £5,000 per pupil).

- Two **bridge courses for year 10** students whose education has broken down. These courses aim to create positive attitudes to education and either re-integrate the young people into mainstream education or prepare them for a year 11 bridge course. The arrangements are similar to the year 11 course, with up to ten pupils on the course at one time with one personal tutor in charge of the programme (cost £5,000 per pupil).

- A **re-integration project** catering for 20 pupils who are not attending mainstream school due to exclusion or long-term non-attendance. The project aims to re-integrate them into school as rapidly as possible by providing temporary programmes to address individual problems and barriers to learning, giving each pupil an agreed target date for full-time transfer and a staged re-integration programme (cost £2,500 per pupil).

- A **GEST training group** to design projects to increase attendance and improve behaviour. In 1994/95, 11 schools participated in schemes to welcome parents to schools; behaviour management; bullying; guidelines for education of children being looked after by the local authority; and counselling skills for education welfare officers.

Evaluation

Attendance at the bridge courses averaged over 80 per cent, in comparison with 39 per cent in the students' previous schools. Ninety per cent of the students who completed the year 11 courses had a positive first destination – with 36 per cent going on to youth training; 10 per cent in employment; and 28 per cent in further education. Students' attitudes to education and employment had improved considerably, as had their self-confidence and esteem. Students' assessment was largely positive, particularly their experience of the teaching and the preparations for independent living.

116. At some sites visited, LEAs were considering paying further education colleges to educate children of 14 and 15 years old who found academic subjects difficult or irrelevant to their needs. However, they were unsure how much to pay for the service, following the transfer of further education colleges out of the LEA sector. In other areas LEAs have reached agreement with further education colleges over the education of 14 and 15 year olds.

117. Joint initiatives between education and social services can also help excluded pupils. In Salford, a special project for children in their last year of school provides part-time education in social services premises, with a high teacher:pupil ratio and an informal atmosphere. The pupils also attend college or work placements for part of the week and in their spare time may receive outward bound training run by a voluntary organisation. Over half of the young people with offending records who attended this course in 1994/95 went on to a job, college or training place, and several more had offers of these. Younger pupils at risk of exclusion are provided with support in school or in other settings, such as a youth club or a public library, for part of the week, by teachers from the joint project. All children who make use of the joint service have time set aside each week to see an individual tutor for counselling and to develop individual action plans.

The education of 'looked after' children

118. Young people who are looked after by local authorities often have educational problems too. Many fail to receive a full-time education. Local audits following the Commission study, *Seen But Not Heard* (Ref. 82), found that nearly half of the children of school age living in local authority residential homes were not attending school on the day that the auditor called and over one-third were not receiving any formal education. The main reasons for their non-attendance at school were being excluded or refusing to attend (Exhibit 47). Between two-thirds and three-quarters of young people leave care with

Exhibit 47
Why were children in residential care not at school?

The main reasons were being excluded or refusing to attend.

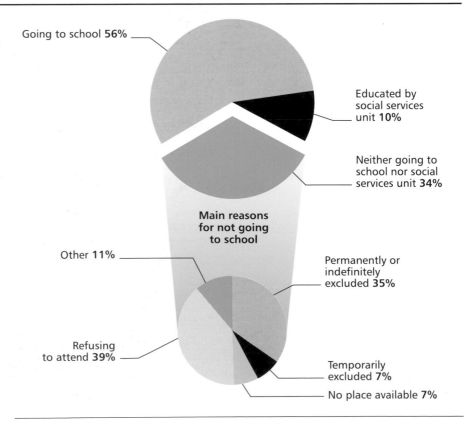

Going to school **56%**

Educated by social services unit **10%**

Neither going to school nor social services unit **34%**

Main reasons for not going to school

Other **11%**

Permanently or indefinitely excluded **35%**

Refusing to attend **39%**

Temporarily excluded **7%**

No place available **7%**

Source: Audit Commission survey

no formal educational qualifications, compared with 18 per cent nationally (Ref. 107). The proportion without qualifications is higher among those leaving residential than foster care and among those who experienced frequent moves. Social services and LEAs should work together to ensure that the educational needs of young people of school age who are accommodated by the local authority in residential homes and elsewhere are met.

Friends and leisure time

119. Young people are influenced by their family and friends. One of the main reasons for committing crime, according to the young offenders who were interviewed, is having family members or friends who offend (Exhibit 48). Most said that they spend much of their leisure time at home or at friends' homes. Another self-report study found that boys who said they had friends who committed offences were eight times more likely than others to admit to offending (Ref. 108). Young people frequently offend in groups of two or three, rather than alone (Ref. 59). Having delinquent friends reinforces any predisposition towards crime and makes it more difficult to break out of a pattern of offending behaviour.

Exhibit 48
Main reasons young offenders give for their behaviour

One of the main reasons given for offending is having family or friends who offend.

Why do you offend?

Family or friends 41%

No money 24%

Alcohol/drugs 10%
Nothing to do 10%
Greed/excitement 9%
Other 4%
Bullied/violence 1%
Stress 1%

Source: Audit Commission survey of 103 young people on supervision orders

Youth work

120. Young people at risk can be encouraged to mix with others who behave responsibly, if they engage in constructive activities, such as sport. Mentoring schemes, in which older people provide role models, can also be helpful. Positive, affordable leisure opportunities also help. Youth clubs and services are important to many young people: 40 per cent of the young offenders interviewed had some contact with youth workers and 20 per cent considered them to be important.

121. The resources devoted to youth work vary widely between authorities in level (Exhibit 49) and in the way in which they are used. Local authorities are required to provide 'an adequate service' for the personal development of young people, through informal social education (Ref. 109). This leaves great scope for local interpretation in coverage, target age group, priorities, staffing, facilities and methods of youth services. Most youth workers view their role as providing a universal service to young people and are unwilling to target their efforts on areas of high deprivation or on those at risk of offending, despite the fact that only one in five 13-19 year olds participates in youth services in England (Ref. 110). Youth service staff in some local authorities are fully occupied running youth clubs which are not necessarily in areas of high deprivation. In other authorities, a deliberately flexible approach has been taken, in which short-term projects are developed, which can respond to the changing needs and lifestyles of young people.

122. Some outdoor adventure activities can improve self-esteem and help to socialise young people, discouraging offending by those at risk. School- or community-based programmes can help to reduce school failure, bullying,

Exhibit 49
Expenditure per head of 11-16 year old population

The resources devoted to youth work vary widely between authorities in level and in the way in which they are used.

Source: CIPFA

Expenditure per head

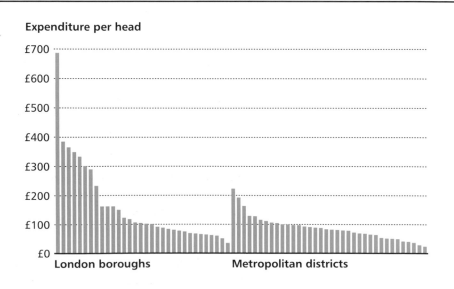

'Where summer activity schemes are provided, it would be more cost effective for youth workers to run them than the police...'

teenage pregnancy, intra-family conflict and removal to residential care. The most successful at reducing offending:

◆ promote a positive and responsible self-image;

◆ improve reasoning skills;

◆ help young people to get on with others; and

◆ involve non-offenders (Ref. 111).

Summer activity schemes in deprived areas, run by youth services and police forces in the summer holidays to provide young people with legitimate activities, often at subsidised prices, can help discourage juvenile nuisance and offending. Youth services are well placed to provide them – although no assessment is available of the impact on offending rates of extra spending on youth services. These activities include motor projects in areas of high motorbike and car crime. In other areas, detached youth workers go out to meet young people on their own ground – on the street, in bus shelters, or wherever young people congregate – with the aim of attracting them to youth clubs; providing information; or simply building positive relationships with adults, which the most disadvantaged young people may not have experienced before.

123. Some youth services have developed projects that are targeted on groups with particular needs. In one town, a drop-in facility for homeless young people provides a café with cheap hot food, information on housing, benefits and drugs, and a clothes exchange. There is additional input from a drugs counsellor, who gives practical help and advice to drug users. Another scheme provides a women's group for young single mothers, sessional work with offenders and help with looking for jobs. In other areas, the youth service helps educate school-age children who are excluded or are truanting from school, and engages young people at high risk from drug abuse, homelessness and other problems in drama and poetry workshops, where they learn to work with others and have their achievements recognised by others, often for the first time (Ref. 112). Attempts should be made to evaluate the effects of youth services, whether in terms of helping pupils to return to school, reducing the level of alcohol and drug abuse by young people or reducing the number of calls to the police from the public, complaining of young people causing a nuisance.

124. Youth services should consider focusing their work in the areas of highest deprivation, to help the most vulnerable young people and encourage them to take part in activities which will promote self-esteem and social skills. They should work in conjunction with other agencies towards shared goals, including the prevention of offending and monitor the effects of this work. Where summer activity schemes are provided, it would be more cost effective for youth workers to run them than the police; where there are large numbers of young people not in education, training or work, detached youth workers could be used to gain their trust and guide them back into mainstream institutions.

125. Legitimate leisure activities for young people are often expensive. To hire sports facilities such as football pitches or badminton courts (at around £4 an hour) can cost more than an evening on drugs or alcohol (at £1 for a bottle of alcoholic lemonade). Private contractors running leisure centres for profit may prefer not to have young people with little money using the facilities that they manage. But young people are more likely to annoy others if they have to create their own diversions than if local communities ensure that suitable options are available. The youth service should provide a directory of activities available to young people, which should include counselling and information services. Voluntary organisations that provide organised activities for young people should be encouraged. Local authorities should consider developing mentoring schemes for vulnerable young people – not only those who offend – that can be costed and monitored.

126. Voluntary organisations can provide some appropriate leisure activities for young people and opportunities to mix with others in a constructive setting. One which works with young people in deprived inner city areas is the Weston Spirit project (Box L). Another is Dance in Action, which provides dance classes for young people in deprived areas of Newcastle-upon-Tyne and Cleveland (Box M).

Box L
The Weston Spirit

The Weston Spirit works in three inner-city areas, to encourage 16 and 17 year olds to engage in positive and constructive activities, and provide them with information and assistance in finding employment or training. The scheme in Newcastle assists around 70 young people each year, at a cost of £1,500 per person. Its income is mainly from trusts and donations, with about 15 per cent from government grants. Many of the participants have been excluded from school or been persistent truants; most have been abusing drugs and 65 per cent have been cautioned or convicted for offending. Potential new members are approached through youth clubs, schools, outreach workers and via word of mouth, from their friends.

Those interested in joining attend an introductory day, followed by a residential week in which they engage in team-building games and outdoor activities and learn to get along with others. Most of the time is spent talking with others or sharing tasks, such as cooking. For most of the participants, this is their first time away from their home environment. After this, members use the centre for educational and social programmes such as how to construct a CV, developing enterprise skills, drama, art and voluntary work. Members can always call in for advice or counselling, or to use the information resource. Many of them become involved in community action with groups such as disadvantaged children or elderly people. All of their achievements are accredited towards a City and Guilds qualification.

Since the scheme began in 1987, 90 per cent of members have gone on to something positive: 42 per cent into employment and 47 per cent to further education. A national evaluation, which received replies from 30 per cent of ex-members, found that only 5 per cent subsequently offended.

Box M
Dance in Action

The scheme reaches 170 young people, both girls and boys, between the ages of nine and 17. It is funded through City Challenge and charitable funds, costing £200,000 over three years. Some of the participants are known offenders, referred by probation or social services; others have been recruited by workers on the streets. If they wish to participate, they are asked to attend a full programme, which lasts from eight to 12 weeks. Although the scheme is optional, attendance figures average over 70 per cent, generally being higher among the older participants and the boys.

The young people learn physical co-ordination, shared with others, which builds their confidence and sense of achievement. Most young people find that they can relate easily to dance, being an everyday component of rock and pop culture. Working towards a performance is an important motivator; they also attend national festivals and share platforms alongside other young people from more advantaged backgrounds. Their parents are invited to performances and are encouraged to take an interest in their children's progress, which is unusual for many. Some of the young people are themselves parents, or are responsible for young siblings, and appreciate the chance to have a specialist activity for themselves. Some of the course participants have been accepted on to further education courses in dance, and most have significantly raised their life expectations and attitudes.

Housing

127. Young people living in unstable conditions are more likely to offend. Over one-third of the young people on supervision orders interviewed by the Audit Commission were not living with a parent (Exhibit 50). Many were living in temporary accommodation, with little support. Those who live at home with parents are less likely to offend and, when they do, are more likely to stop as they get older (Ref. 9). In a number of the sites visited, parents were asking their troublesome children to leave home at age 16, and no agency appeared to be discouraging them. A mother complained that social services had done nothing to help when a stepfather threatened to expel a stepson from home on his sixteenth birthday. In some of the local authorities visited, local housing departments provide accommodation for young people who leave home, despite the wishes of their parents.

Exhibit 50
Where young offenders on supervision orders are living

Over one-third of the young offenders interviewed were not living with a parent.

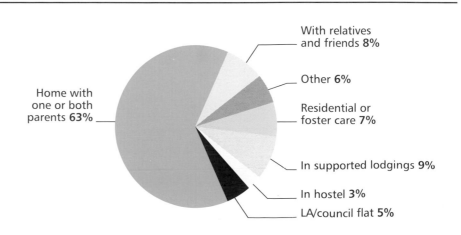

Home with one or both parents **63%**

With relatives and friends **8%**

Other **6%**

Residential or foster care **7%**

In supported lodgings **9%**

In hostel **3%**

LA/council flat **5%**

Source: Audit Commission survey of 103 young people on supervision orders

128. Eighty-six per cent of young people who are homeless leave home because of the breakdown of family relationships, often with step-parents (Ref. 113). Some are told to leave home; others leave because of family disputes or, sometimes, abuse. More than half of those under 18 who ask for help with a housing problem are young women, and most have been staying with friends, sisters, brothers or other relatives (Ref. 114). Young people leaving young offender institutions or probation or bail hostels face particular problems in finding suitable housing. Homeless young people are rarely a priority for housing departments and, if provided with council flats, often find it difficult to maintain their tenancy. Young black people appear to experience even more difficulty and are over-represented among the homeless group (Ref. 115).

Young people leaving care

129. Young people who have been in the care of local authorities are an especially vulnerable group. They tend to move to independent living at a younger age than those who live with their families and most experience difficulties (Refs. 116, 117). Nearly one-third have moved to independent living before their seventeenth birthday and nearly-two thirds by the age of 18. Some of these, however, move to a bedsit or flat before being officially discharged from care, sometimes in a crisis situation when foster or residential placements break down. Others move sooner than they really want, as council flats become available. Most of them continue to move frequently on leaving care, 40 per cent experiencing at least one move and over 10 per cent making four or more moves within the first three to nine months. A survey by those who had left care found that nearly 80 per cent had been totally without money at least once, when benefit cheques failed to arrive or because money had been stolen from them (Ref. 118). Nearly one in seven of the young women in one study were pregnant or were already mothers by the time they left care. Research by Centrepoint (Ref. 113) suggests that many (57 per cent in 1989) young homeless people aged 16-19 had been in social services care at some point in their lives, although most of those who have been in care do not experience problems such as homelessness or offending.

130. The Children Act 1989 requires social services departments to provide support for young people leaving care at age 16 or older. This support might cover help and advice with housing, benefits and employment, training or education, as well as the open-ended emotional support that most families would expect to provide for their children for a considerable period of time.

'Eighty-six per cent of young people who are homeless leave home because of the breakdown of family relationships, often with step-parents.'

131. However, the extent of support for care-leavers varies widely between local authorities (Exhibit 51). A survey of 75 authorities in 1992 showed that half had no written policy or procedure for supporting those who leave care (Ref. 119). Some provide a range of accommodation for young people as they move through the stages to independence, such as hostel provision with attached flats, where people can live semi-independently for some months, with easy access to help and support when required. Others provide furnished flats, with more frequent support, which is gradually withdrawn as the person gains greater confidence. A few provide a drop-in centre in the local town for

Exhibit 51
The budget for support for care-leavers (per number leaving in 1992/93 – includes staff, accommodation, payments to young people, other expenditure)

The extent of support provided varies widely.

Source: Audit Commission survey

Expenditure per head

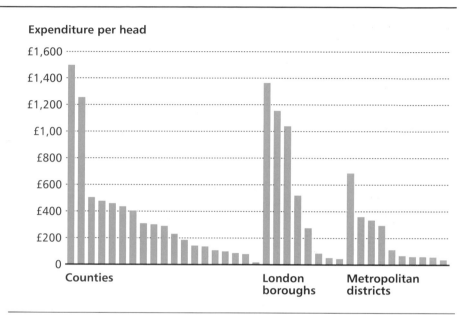

people living independently, and may organise holidays and activities. Some leaving care schemes are managed by voluntary organisations in partnership with the social services department. The best schemes seem to have a flexible range of housing options, including supported lodgings, which are available to young people who need it rather than on the basis of age, and which allow them to return to a more highly supported setting if they need to. These schemes may also provide help in renegotiating relationships with the young person's family. Promoting employment, training and educational opportunities may also be an important element (Ref. 120).

132. A voluntary sector scheme in one authority (run by NCH Action for Children) provides move-on accommodation in supported lodgings for young people who have offended (though it could be equally appropriate for those leaving care). An evaluation of the scheme found that those who had lived in supported lodgings after their initial foster placement had generally led more stable lives and re-offended less. The landlord/landlady received training from NCH and was able to claim an enhanced rate of housing benefit, depending on the individual's level of need or risk (high, medium, low). The changes in housing benefit regulations introduced in January 1996 may lead to this scheme being terminated.

133. Some local authorities provide care for older teenagers, support for care-leavers and youth justice services through the same service. Bexley Social Services has an adolescent resource centre which provides housing and special fostering for challenging adolescents alongside aftercare and youth justice, including work to discourage young offenders from re-offending. Salford has similar arrangements. But in most areas there is a duplication of service; different teams of social workers are looking after care-leavers and young offenders separately, although they are providing equivalent services to these different groups of young people at risk, often with little idea of the cost.

Local authorities should consider providing social services for older teenagers and their families as an integrated service, encompassing flexible support for those leaving care; similar support for the most vulnerable young people aged 16-21, including those thrown out of their parental home; and youth justice services for those up to the age of 18. Children's services plans should encourage planning for vulnerable teenagers and young offenders across agencies. Schemes worth piloting include support groups for parents in the most high-risk areas, to help them cope with teenagers who have particular problems; and foyer schemes, where homeless young people in deprived areas can receive help with training and employment in a residential setting.

Training and employment

134. Boredom and having nothing to do were also major reasons given by young offenders for their behaviour. Sixty per cent of the young offenders on supervision orders interviewed by the Audit Commission had little to do, as they were not engaged in work, training or education (Exhibit 52). Many of them had difficulty in reading and writing. Only 30 per cent of those without a formal occupation mentioned any sports or hobbies.

135. Few young people of 16 and 17 who are not living with a parent attend school or college, while 72 per cent who are living with their parents do so. Those living in institutions are particularly likely to be unemployed (Exhibit 53). Parents should normally be responsible for their children up to the age of 18, in particular for housing them, and be supported by social services where there is a high risk of irrevocable family breakdown. If local authorities accommodate young people under 18, they should consider recovering the costs from those parents who can afford to pay, as the Children Act 1989 requires them to do for children under 16.

136. Many unemployed young people, especially young men, continue to be unemployed into their early 20s. In one area, around 8 per cent of 16 and 17 year olds were not registered in education, training or work (estimated on the basis of registered and unregistered individuals) (Ref. 121). Almost all of them had experienced trouble with the law, drug abuse, violence, physical or sexual abuse, broken homes, or some combination of these. These young people would have a better chance of entering further education, training or

Exhibit 52
Daytime occupation of young offenders on supervision orders

60 per cent of those interviewed were not engaged in work, training or education.

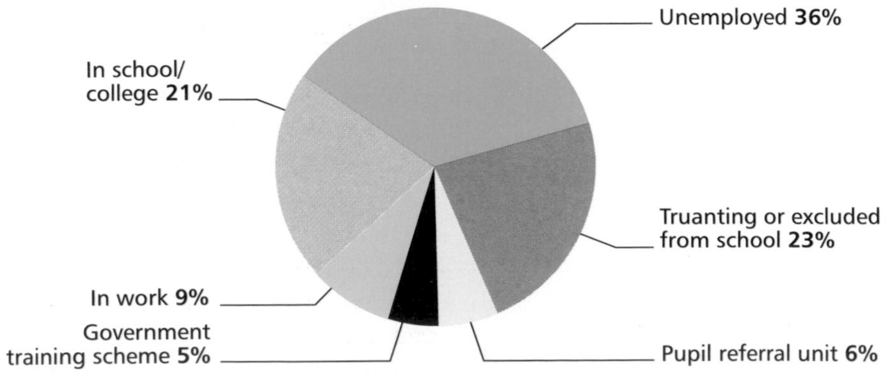

Source: Audit Commission survey of 103 young people on supervision orders

Unemployed **36%**

In school/college **21%**

Truanting or excluded from school **23%**

In work **9%**

Government training scheme **5%**

Pupil referral unit **6%**

Exhibit 53
The daytime occupation of 16 and
17 year olds in England

Those living in institutions are
particularly likely to be unemployed.

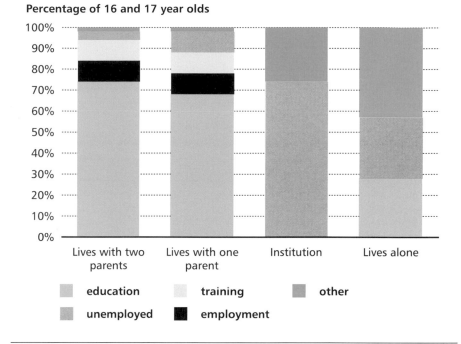

Percentage of 16 and 17 year olds

education   training   other

unemployed   employment

Source: Youth Cohort Study, cohort 7, sweep 1

employment if careers advice for every range of ability were made available to
them. The careers service draws up an action plan for all school-leavers two
years before they leave, recording their achievements, goals and training needs.
Many of the young offenders interviewed had been absent from school for
much of their last two years and so had missed out on advice from the careers
service. The careers service could fulfil a useful role in helping those young
people who are not involved in education, training or work if it made
systematic attempts to contact all of this group. Youth services, working
alongside the careers service, could help to identify individuals who need their
help and assist them to use the service. Young people who get to
school-leaving age without being able to read and write should be offered
specific help to develop their literacy skills.

Training courses

137. Most of the funding for local Training and Enterprise Councils (TECs) is
allocated according to the number of trainees that they succeed in helping into
employment or to gain qualifications, leaving little incentive to train those
who are less able – including young offenders and young people with poor
educational records. Some special funding is available for schemes to assist
those who have been unemployed for long periods of time or who have special
needs. But there is little money available, for instance, for training to NVQ
level 1. The Government intends that training opportunities be available for
all school-leavers, but this has proved difficult to achieve, as matching
individual needs to placements can be a problem. Training should reflect the
skills and abilities of young people who aspire to provide essential services to
local people, including hairdressing, painting and decorating, gardening,

cleaning and personal caring, as well as the needs of local employers who require other skills. Priority should be given to reviewing the range of training, basic qualifications and employment options for less able young people – to divert them from the temptation to commit crime.

138. Where no training course is available for young people out of education and employment, discretionary severe hardship payments are available. Factors taken into account include health and vulnerability, the threat of homelessness, the prospects of speedy entry into youth training and the availability of casual work (Ref. 122). To claim severe hardship payments, a young person has to register for training with the careers service, take proof of registration to the employment service and, finally, attend the local Benefits Agency office for interview. Many of the youth justice and voluntary workers interviewed by the Commission spend a considerable amount of time helping young people through this process. Simplifying the process would therefore help both young people in severe hardship and those who help them.

139. Unemployed young people who undertake voluntary work may lose any social security benefits that they are receiving if the local job centre does not accept that they are still actively seeking work. Voluntary work can help young people to develop skills and experience as well as providing references for job applications. Young people out of education and training and on benefits should be allowed and encouraged to participate in voluntary work – to help others and to develop skills that they can subsequently sell.

140. Policies to reduce crime by young men may have only limited success while large numbers continue to be without work, unless general attitudes to work change. Every effort should be made to reduce unemployment among young people by educating and training every young person to a level where they are able to perform useful jobs, including caring and looking after the vulnerable. The proposed development of a vocational curriculum for 14-16 year olds may help with this. Encouraging parents to house their children up to the age of 18 may also help.

141. In some cases, it may not be possible for children to live with their parents. 'Foyers' – hostels which provide an integrated approach to housing, training and employment – have had some success in reaching young people who are homeless and unemployed. These are based on a model which has been in operation for some time in France (Box N).

Box N
Foyers

Foyer schemes are funded from a variety of sources, including the employment service, TECs, Single Regeneration Budget (SRB), the Housing Corporation and other grants. Foyer staff can provide assistance with training, employment and personal issues in a less formal manner than can most government programmes. One-quarter of the residents are aged 15 to 17, most of the remainder being under 25. Two-thirds are male and one-third female. Up to one-third have been in trouble with the police. In the first two years, 1,800 people went through the foyer programme, 55 per cent finding jobs and 18 per cent going into training (Ref. 123). The average length of stay was about six months, with a maximum of two to three years. The unit cost was approximately £1,500 per positive outcome (which compares favourably with the £2,500 to process a young offender through court).

Box O
Self-build schemes for young people

Self-build schemes assist young unemployed people to build their own homes. The young people receive assistance from development workers and volunteers and have to learn to work as a team and be reliable. This provides suitable discipline and helps them to acquire social, technical and administrative skills. In one programme, consisting of nine schemes initiated by Charity Projects funding, 67 young people have so far participated and 103 bed spaces have been provided (Ref. 124). Other schemes, using funding from housing associations, local firms and charitable trusts, have succeeded in building several thousand living units. The Young Builders' Trust, for example, works with the local authority, housing associations, probation services and TECs to provide training in building, with NVQ qualifications. These can help to enhance young people's future employment prospects as well as providing homes for them.

142. There are a number of ways in which young people can be assisted to gain skills needed for employment, such as self-build schemes (Box O).

Drugs and alcohol

143. The use of alcohol and other drugs is high among young offenders, compared with other young people. Almost half of the 16-19 year old young men questioned in the 1994 British Crime Survey used illegal drugs at some point in their lives (Ref. 125). But 70 per cent of the 103 young offenders on supervision orders interviewed by the Audit Commission said that they took drugs of some kind and 9 per cent had tried heroin at least once (Exhibit 54, overleaf). Twenty-three per cent said that their offending had sometimes been influenced by the need to take drugs, as they had spent some of the proceeds in this way, although 77 per cent saw no connection. Some described the use of a shared kitty to buy alcohol and other drugs for evenings out, leading to group pressure to participate in their use. A study in Leicester of young people aged 13-16 found that those who used drugs more frequently were also more likely to have committed a large number of offences, but that the activities were relatively independent of each other (Ref. 126).

144. Fifty per cent of the young offenders interviewed said that they got drunk at least once a week (Exhibit 54, overleaf), and 44 per cent said that a parent or someone else in the family home got drunk regularly. Several said that their father was drunk nearly every night.

145. In an Audit Commission survey, 15 per cent of 600 young people sentenced by a court were judged by their youth justice worker to have a problem with either drugs or alcohol (Exhibit 55, overleaf). The chances of male offenders desisting from crime are considerably lower if they are heavy drinkers or use hard drugs (Ref. 9).

Exhibit 54
Use of drugs and alcohol by young
offenders on supervision orders

Seventy per cent take drugs of some kind...

Type of drug

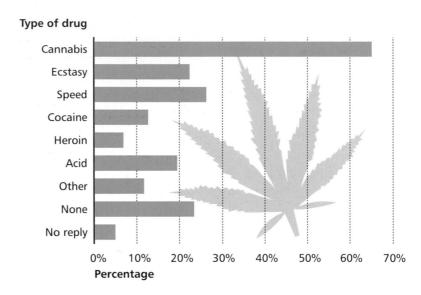

...and half of them get drunk every week.

Frequency of getting drunk

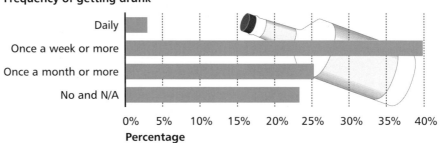

*Source: Audit Commission survey of 103 young
people on supervision orders*

Exhibit 55
Drug and alcohol problems in
sentenced offenders

Fifteen per cent of young people sentenced
by the court were described as having a
problem with drugs or alcohol.

Percentage with problem

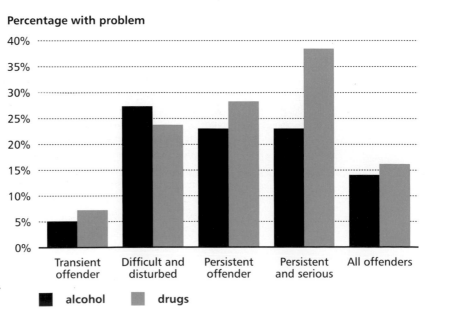

*Source: Audit Commission survey. Classification of
offender types from Little (Ref. 11)*

Help with drug and alcohol problems

146. Facilities for helping young offenders, and other young people, with problems of alcohol or drug abuse vary in different parts of the country. In the London Borough of Brent, a range of facilities for educating and treating those under the age of 18 with drug and alcohol problems have been developed, using the resources of voluntary and statutory sectors (Box P). These have been developed as part of a multi-agency strategy, similar in approach to that of a Drug Action Team, as required by the Government's strategy, 'Tackling Drugs Together'.

Box P
Addressing the drug problems of young people in Brent

One voluntary organisation, Agapay, provides a high street café with counselling and a needle exchange and another, Turning Point, provides counselling and outreach work which is aimed particularly at young people.

An outreach youth worker runs sessions in a number of GP practices in areas of high deprivation and drug problems. These sessions cost £25,000 per year, which is provided by a grant from the Standing Conference on Drug Abuse (SCODA). One hundred and fifty people were seen for assessment or consultation in the first nine months. The scheme has been extended to other venues, such as housing estates and an information shop, where young people are more comfortable talking about sensitive issues and do not feel that they are being 'checked up on'. Health visitors have proved to be an important source of referrals and are likely to remain the key point of contact with health centres. In addition, a GP who has been trained in dealing with drug users is providing training to other GPs and primary care teams in the borough.

A peer education project has been established for two years in two areas of the borough, with funding from City Challenge and the Single Regeneration Budget. It costs around £28,000 for staff, materials and volunteer expenses. Each year, 20 young people between the ages of 15 and 25 are trained to provide information and advice on drug-related issues to their peers; each is expected to make two contacts per month. The success of the scheme has so far led to proposals to extend it across the borough and into neighbouring Harrow, using European Community funds.

A family support programme has been established to provide parents, relatives and friends of drug users with information, counselling and practical help. In the first six months 114 contacts were made, mainly by telephone, with 14 people becoming regular clients. A separate hotline has also been established, on a 24-hour, seven-day a week basis, for parents who are concerned about their children. In nine months 100 calls were received; most related to general antisocial behaviour, but 18 related specifically to drugs. Over half were referred on to other agencies for further help. A schools education initiative, Theatre in Education, which received GEST funding, used drama, dance, music and circus skills to raise awareness among primary school children. Each programme comprised ten weekly sessions which required participation and questioning on the part of the pupils. The evaluation indicated a greater understanding of the effects of drugs, awareness of how to deal with peer pressure and more willingness to help out friends in trouble.

147. Since heavy use of drugs and alcohol is associated with persistent offending, it should be addressed as part of a court sentence or caution plus action plan. Drug Action Teams should ensure that strategies for those with drug and alcohol problems cater for the needs of young people under the age of 18.

Reinforcing community institutions

148. Understanding right and wrong is a major determinant of behaviour. When asked what would stop them, if tempted to steal, most young people said 'because it is wrong' (Exhibit 56). Learning to be responsible is an important part of growing up and ceasing to engage in antisocial behaviour such as offending. Desisting from offending is, for females, associated with entering stable relationships with the opposite sex; forming new families and becoming economically independent, socially responsible and self-reliant. For males, however, it seems that these responsibilities have no effect, at least not before the age of 25. For males, the only factors associated with desisting from offending were their perception that their school work was above average and continuing to live at home (Ref. 9).

149. Some young people seem to fail to learn the distinction between right and wrong. If people are not tolerant and respectful of others, or do not abide by the laws of the country, strong, coercive and expensive sanctions will be needed to keep order (Ref. 127). Success in passing on social norms and traditions to produce trustworthy young people will tend to reduce crime and, correspondingly, the need to spend money protecting property and punishing dishonest behaviour. Communities which succeed in this task will have an advantage over others. All public services should co-operate with institutions that socialise young people – such as families, schools, religious institutions and community organisations – to ensure that children have the opportunity to become responsible and capable citizens.

Exhibit 56
The reason for not offending, if tempted (in young people of 14-25)

Most young people do not steal because they believe that such actions are wrong.

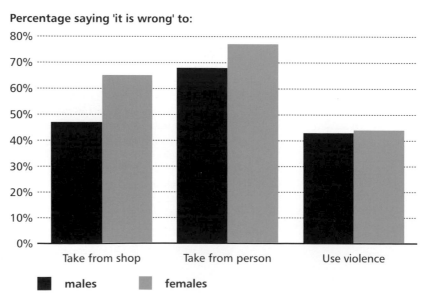

Percentage saying 'it is wrong' to:

Source: Graham and Bowling (1995, unpublished)

88

Conclusions

' Parents have the first and most important role in ensuring that their children grow up to respect authority and to be concerned about the wellbeing of others.'

150. There is a high degree of consensus on the factors associated with offending, and a number of promising interventions have been identified – ranging from family centres to better training for employment. Local agencies need to pilot schemes which use these interventions in the areas where they are most needed, and to evaluate them to learn what works (Exhibit 57, overleaf).

151. Preventing youth crime is the responsibility of a wide range of agencies and individuals. Parents have the first and most important role in ensuring that their children grow up to respect authority and to be concerned about the wellbeing of others. Public agencies – such as social services, health visitors, nursery schools and voluntary organisations – can help them in this task. That help is most likely to be useful if it is focused on the neighbourhoods with the greatest needs and where the costs and effects of schemes are monitored and evaluated. Support for those with problems at school, especially in the areas of highest risk, should also link with the family. Sixteen and seventeen year olds should be: encouraged to live with one or both parents; helped to engage in constructive leisure activities; and encouraged to take up training towards employment. The criminal justice system and other support services should be component parts of a system for reinforcing authority and providing positive opportunities. In this way, the cycle of antisocial behaviour can be broken and young people helped to achieve their potential and play a full part in society.

Exhibit 57
Breaking into the cycle of antisocial behaviour

Local agencies need to pilot schemes which use these promising interventions in the areas where they are most needed, and to evaluate them to learn what works.

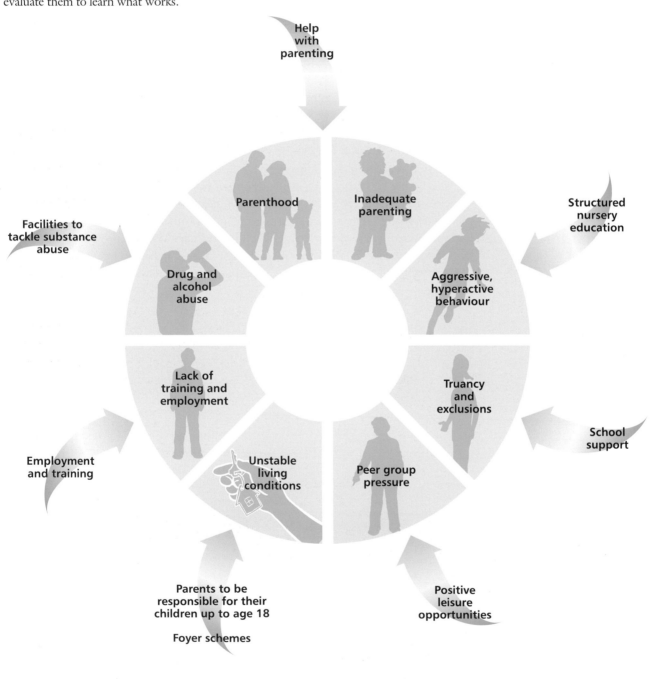

Source: Audit Commission

Recommendations

Helping with parenting

1 In conjunction with education, health visitors and mental health services, social services should consider piloting schemes in deprived areas to provide guidance on parenting, and assistance to those with difficulties through family centres and volunteer programmes.

- Promising options include: multi-agency family centres – which may include social workers, health visitors or volunteer projects – in deprived neighbourhoods; and volunteer programmes that link new parents living in high-risk areas with experienced parents who are able to offer practical help and support for an hour or two a week – along the lines of the Homestart and Newpin programmes. In high-risk areas that do not have family centres, social services and health services should consider piloting such programmes.

- Health visitors are likely to have a key role in identifying the local areas and families which may be most at risk.

- Child and adolescent mental health services should ensure that they have expertise in dealing with conduct disorders. Mental health professionals should place greater priority on indirect work, supporting health visitors, family centres and voluntary groups when they are dealing with children whose behaviour is difficult – and should monitor the effects of this work. As part of their commissioning process, health commissioning authorities should specify support to these groups in their contracts with mental health providers, and monitoring and evaluation.

Structured nursery schooling

2 LEAs should consider targeting schemes to provide intensive, structured pre-school education and home support for three and four your olds, in which parents are involved, to areas of high risk and deprivation; and they should be evaluated. Providers of pre-school education should consider helping parents to reinforce the discipline that they teach.

School support

3
- Schools, with the help of education support services, should reinforce good behaviour, encouraging the involvement of parents.

- Child mental health services should offer support to teachers in schools dealing with pupils with behaviour problems, particularly those in high-risk areas. Health commissioners need to ensure that contracts with healthcare providers specify pilot programmes designed to advise and assist schools dealing with pupils with behavioural problems in areas of high risk and deprivation, and evaluate their effects.

◆ LEAs should, as part of their community safety strategy, consider encouraging schools to develop strategies for addressing truancy where absenteeism is high, drawing on good practice promoted by the DfEE, and monitoring their effects. The police and other local services should help to evaluate the impact of such schemes on juvenile nuisance and offending by young people.

◆ Where pupils are excluded, LEAs should require schools to confirm that their special educational needs have been fully considered.

◆ Social services could pilot the attachment of family support workers to schools in deprived areas, to help keep young people at risk in school.

◆ LEAs should promote the re-integration of excluded children into school. They should consider commissioning independent agencies, such as Cities in Schools, in areas with particular problems, to help disaffected pupils return to schools, and to provide effective alternatives for pupils out of school.

◆ Social services and LEAs should work together to ensure that the educational needs of young people of school age who are accommodated by the local authority in residential homes and elsewhere are met.

Positive leisure opportunities

4 Youth services should consider focusing their work in the areas of highest deprivation, to help the most vulnerable young people and encourage them to take part in activities that will promote self-esteem and social skills. They should:

◆ work in conjunction with other agencies towards shared goals, including the prevention of offending and monitor the effects of this work. Where summer activity schemes are provided, it would be more cost effective for youth workers to run them than the police; where there are large numbers of young people not in education, training or work, detached youth workers could be used to gain their trust and guide them back into mainstream institutions;

◆ provide a directory of activities available to young people which should include counselling and information services;

◆ encourage voluntary organisations that provide organised activities for young people.

5 Local authorities should consider developing mentoring schemes for vulnerable young people in deprived areas – not only those who offend – that can be costed and monitored.

Housing needs and leaving care

6   Local authorities should consider providing social services for older teenagers as an integrated service, encompassing flexible support for those leaving care; similar support for the most vulnerable young people aged 16-21, including those thrown out of their parental home; and youth justice services for those up to the age of 18. Children's services plans should encourage planning for vulnerable teenagers and young offenders across agencies.

7   Schemes worth piloting include support groups for parents in the most high-risk areas; and foyer schemes, where homeless young people in deprived areas can receive help with training and employment in a residential setting.

8   Parents should normally be responsible for their children up to the age of 18, in particular for housing them, and be supported by social services where there is a high risk of irrevocable family breakdown. If local authorities accommodate young people under 18, they should consider recovering the costs from those parents who can afford to pay.

Employment and training opportunities

9   The careers service could fulfil a useful role in helping those young people who are not involved in education, training or work if it made systematic attempts to contact all of this group. Youth services, working alongside the careers service, could help to identify those individuals who need their help and assist them to use the service.

10   Young people who get to school-leaving age without being able to read and write should be offered specific help to develop their literacy skills.

11   Young people out of education and training and on benefits should be allowed and encouraged to participate in voluntary work – to help others and to develop skills that they can subsequently sell.

12   Every effort should be made to reduce unemployment among young people by educating and training every young person to a level where they are able to perform useful jobs, including caring and looking after the vulnerable.

Drugs and alcohol

13 Since heavy use of drugs and alcohol is associated with persistent offending, it should be addressed as part of a court sentence or caution plus action plan. Drug Action Teams should ensure that strategies for those with drug and alcohol problems cater for the needs of young people under the age of 18.

Reinforcing community institutions

14 All public services should co-operate with institutions that socialise young people – such as families, schools, religious institutions and community organisations – to ensure that children have the opportunity to become responsible and capable citizens.

Local authority chief executives should consider initiating forums, involving all relevant departments and agencies, to develop local strategies for addressing and preventing youth crime. All the participants should share information needed to identify problems and evaluate interventions.

Central government can help by co-ordinating the advice given by departments to different local services; and by considering how savings from the more efficient processing of young offenders can best be transferred to more effective measures for dealing with offenders and preventing offending in the first place.

3 Developing a Strategy

Why a strategy is needed

152. The current system for dealing with youth crime is inefficient and expensive, while little is being done to deal effectively with juvenile nuisance. The present arrangements are failing the young people – who are not being guided away from offending to constructive activities. They are also failing victims – those who suffer from some young people's inconsiderate behaviour, and from vandalism, arson and loss of property from thefts and burglaries. And they lead to waste in a variety of forms, including lost time, as public servants process the same young offenders through the courts time and again; lost rents, as people refuse to live in high crime areas; lost business, as people steer clear of troubled areas; and the waste of young people's potential.

153. Resources need to be shifted from processing young offenders to dealing with their behaviour. At the same time, efforts to prevent offending and other antisocial behaviour by young people need to be co-ordinated between the different agencies involved; they should also be targeted on deprived areas with high crime rates, and piloted and evaluated (Exhibit 58).

Exhibit 58
Changing the emphasis

Resources need to be shifted from processing young offenders to dealing with their behaviour.

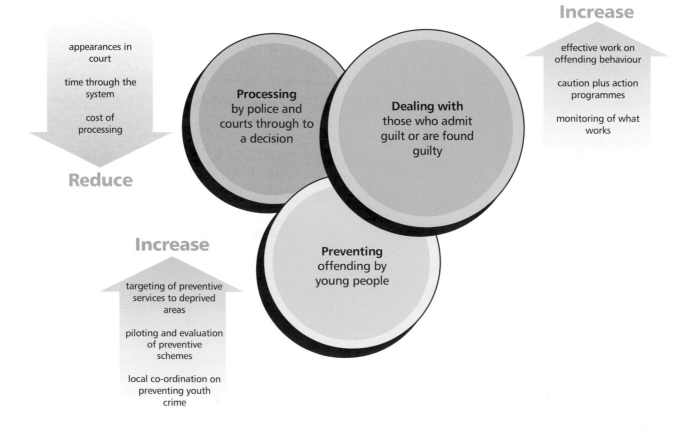

Source: Audit Commission

154. This shift in resources in resources can be achieved by:

(i) streamlining current processes –

– minimising the paperwork required of police officers when a young person is prosecuted;

– reducing the length of time between arrest of a young offender and sentencing in court; and

– reducing the average number of appearances in court required before a young offender is sentenced.

(ii) dealing more effectively with known offenders using –

– 'caution plus' action programmes for young people whose offending behaviour is not yet entrenched;

– more intensive supervision programmes for those persistent offenders who are given community sentences, teaching them new ways to behave and skills to help them into education, training or employment; and

– monitoring rates of re-offending after different court sentences and caution plus schemes to learn from experience which are most effective at reducing recidivism.

(iii) piloting and evaluating preventive programmes which are targeted on deprived areas with high levels of antisocial behaviour by children and young people and which –

– work with parents in family centres and, through voluntary schemes, put new parents in touch with experienced ones;

– help schools to deal better with disruptive pupils, avoiding exclusions where possible and reducing truanting;

– encourage mental health services to offer guidance and support to teachers who are dealing with pupils with behavioural problems;

– attach family support workers to schools in deprived areas;

– focus youth services on the most deprived areas, to help vulnerable young people to develop self-esteem and social skills;

– provide 'foyers' – hostels which provide an integrated approach to housing, training and employment for homeless young people;

– give priority to the training and employment options for less able young people; and

– ensure that services developed locally by Drug Action Teams are available to those under 18 with substance abuse problems.

Co-ordinating programmes to prevent youth crime and other antisocial behaviour

155. A strategy involving all of these steps requires action by a wide range of agencies – and this action must be co-ordinated if it is to have greatest effect. This, in turn, requires a framework. Existing structures are best used wherever possible, as they have procedures and networks of contacts already in place. Local government provides one such structure which spans youth justice services (social services), education, youth services, leisure services, and housing. Local authorities already have a duty under the Children Act 1989 (schedule 2 section 7b) to take steps to encourage children in their area not to commit criminal offences. Some are unitary authorities, responsible for the full range of local authority services, while others operate within a two-tier system and must therefore undertake additional co-ordination.

156. Area Criminal Justice Liaison Committees (ACJLCs), on the other hand, are chaired by judges and provide co-ordination across court services. But they cover large geographical areas, and not all the agencies that are based within an area are represented. As ACJLCs have to rely on members to represent colleagues in neighbouring authorities, or different services within the same local authority, they do not bring all the relevant parties together. At the managerial level, youth courts usually run multi-agency court user groups and these are the appropriate forums in which to discuss the business of the court. But these groups do not usually discuss policy, and exclude many of the preventive services.

157. It may, therefore, be necessary to establish some wider forum that brings together local government and the youth courts with the police, probation and health services. One agency should be seen as responsible for initiating action. A survey of local authorities found that, while 63 per cent already participate in such groups, the main barrier to community safety work, after funding, was lack of statutory powers (Ref. 128). To provide a local focus, local authority chief executives should consider initiating forums in which all relevant local authority departments and other agencies participate. While the main focus of these forums would be to develop a strategy to prevent youth crime, they could also oversee any multi-agency caution plus schemes and develop wider community safety plans. They should give priority to areas where crime, juvenile nuisance and the risks of offending are high, and to co-ordinating a local response. The most effective schemes – such as the Northamptonshire Diversion Unit (see Box E) – occur where authorities already promote multi-agency co-ordination.

158. A local forum on its own is not sufficient. It will need to translate into action at three levels:

◆ **the strategic level:** policymakers need to determine the scope for collaboration and set objectives for joint action, in the light of past and present initiatives and local problems. In Northamptonshire, the chief officers of all services dealing with young people meet regularly to discuss joint initiatives and to inform each other of any changes to their services that may impact on the work of others. Policymakers should ensure that managers and practitioners are able and willing to share information, to

' To provide a local focus, local authority chief executives should consider initiating forums in which all relevant local authority departments and other agencies participate.'

help identify areas where young people are causing problems and to help develop services that address those problems.

- **the management level:** managers need to reflect the objectives set by policymakers when they allocate resources and set priorities for staff. One approach is to establish an interagency group for each neighbourhood that is identified by the policymakers as a priority area. This group can consider how best to identify residents' needs and practical ways of addressing them, making sure that local residents – including young people – have the opportunity to contribute their views.

- **the practitioner level:** practitioners need to see the value of the multi-agency approach and to understand the aims of other services dealing with young people. Joint training of practitioners working in particular areas can help promote shared understanding. In many cases, practitioners find that they are dealing with different aspects of problems presented by the same families.

159. As a minimum, local authorities should ensure that they have strategies, formulated and agreed by all the relevant services, in the context of children's services plans, for encouraging children in their areas not to commit criminal offences. But once established, local forums could act as a focus for community safety initiatives that go wider than the issues covered in this report – considering, for example, how to improve community safety by reducing opportunities for crime and making it more difficult. Consultation with police authorities before finalising local community safety plans would be important, in order to ensure that any community safety plans are consistent with the annual policing plans produced by police authorities. Community safety will continue to be crucial. The Commission intends to return to the issue within the next few years, to examine how it is being promoted within local authorities.

Sharing information

160. Developing a strategy could start by sharing information to identify the local areas at highest risk, as some will be at greater risk than others. Over 40 per cent of crime against individuals is concentrated in 10 per cent of neighbourhoods (Exhibit 7), so preventive work should be focused on these areas. Local authority departments, such as housing and social services, can contribute information about which areas experience the worst problems of crime and nuisance. Census information, available by enumeration districts which cover around 200 households, can also provide information on local conditions and social factors which are associated with a risk of young people drifting into offending. The police have a particularly important role in identifying where most of the crime and nuisance by young people is taking place.

161. Services are often reluctant to share information about offending by individuals, before or after conviction: one youth justice service visited considered it wrong to inform education services of court actions against children for fear that it would prejudice the school against them. Professional ethics are sometimes cited as an impediment to the free flow of information. Others cite the Data Protection Act 1984 – though this does not prevent services sharing information in some parts of England and Wales. The Act allows social services and probation to receive certain kinds of information from the police. Effective communication depends on local relationships and a willingness to work together. All agencies should ensure that they have taken the necessary steps to share any relevant information with others who are dealing with young offenders.

Practical solutions

Focus on deprived areas

162. Residents of the areas at highest risk, including the young people themselves, should be consulted about the problems they face. Any possible solutions that have been identified should also be discussed, drawing on what works elsewhere. There is no panacea – local problems will vary, as will the most appropriate solutions – but there is a high degree of consensus on the factors associated with offending. The most useful interventions will address the risk factors known to be associated with offending. A leisure centre may be appropriate in one area, and detached youth work coupled with housing projects in another. In other areas, the needs of families with young children may be most acute, indicating the need for better family support and structured nursery education. Some examples of strategic and operational approaches to preventing youth crime are outlined below. The approach taken in France involves a wide range of agencies, working in conjunction with local communities (Box Q).

Box Q
Preventing juvenile offending in France

France has an elaborate structure for crime prevention at national, regional and local levels. Most medium-size towns have a committee for delinquency prevention, including representatives of the police and other key agencies. The responsibility for social crime prevention is shared by many, largely non-criminal justice agencies such as schools, youth clubs and families. Mainstream agencies are seen to be more relevant than special projects in integrating disaffected young people. In addition, teams of special neighbourhood-based prevention workers – who are quite separate from the justice system and often act as advocates for the young people – contact those who may be at risk, establish their trust and aim to lead them back into mainstream institutions. Much of their work takes place on the street. They may need to develop special activities and venues in the process, such as boxing clubs, music cafés, parents' groups (to encourage interest in education), and homework clubs. The residents of local areas, including young people themselves, are given ownership of the problem of youth crime and the authority to influence decisions. In addition, large preventive schemes have a high profile nationally.

Strategic co-ordination

163. Northamptonshire provides a good example of strategic co-ordination working in practice. The chief officers of all agencies dealing with young people are represented on an InterDependency Group (IDG) (Exhibit 59). They exchange information, discuss issues of mutual concern, and consult each other before implementing changes in one service that may affect others. This enables some sharing of resources where this is mutually beneficial. The chair rotates every two years. Co-operation in the IDG is now reinforced by community safety groups at district council level and by local action against crime groups. A county community safety officer co-ordinates activity within the framework of a community safety plan.

Bottom-up co-ordination

164. Other local authorities have taken a different approach which does not depend on the services sharing coterminous boundaries. Salford has adopted a 'bottom-up' approach to interagency co-operation which focuses on local areas (Box R, overleaf).

Exhibit 59
Membership of the Northamptonshire IDG

The chief officers of all the agencies dealing with young people are involved in an InterDependency Group.

InterDependency group	County
- Chief Executive County Council	
- Police - Probation - Magistrates Clerk	
- Social Services - Education - Prison Service	
- CPS - Crown and County Courts - Health Authority	

Community safety groups	District
- Housing	
- Leisure and Recreation	
Action against crime groups	
Project groups	

Community consultative committees	Local
- Public consultation	

Source: Northamptonshire County Council

In Salford, some local authority chief officers co-ordinate corporate and interagency activity – in addition to their other duties – in particular parts of the city. The Eccles group, chaired by the director of social services, includes representatives from the police, probation and the community as well as from housing, education and youth services. Areas of Eccles suffer multiple incidents of vandalism and other crimes. Youths on the street complained of a lack of facilities and having nothing to do, while nearby a small open space was fouled, littered and used as a dump for stolen cars. A local survey showed a high level of apathy, with people staying at home and tolerating crime. The survey was followed up by a meeting with local residents where the main complaint concerned problems with young people.

Acting together, the agencies organised a Fun Day in which 1,500 local residents turned up to enjoy a funfair and barbecue. A clean-up was organised. A residents' association was formed with help from social services, housing and the police. Schools were persuaded to open their halls to outside groups. A database of activities in the area was established so that all agencies, including the police, could guide young people towards activities that interest them. Community safety funding was obtained to establish the multidisciplinary Eccles Youth Project, which employs 11 part-time workers to work with young people in the area. Seven groups have been targeted: five are geographically defined in order to reach areas of high crime and deprivation; one is for young women; and one for young black and Asian men.

Strategy for young people

165. Elsewhere, young people have been formally involved in a community safety strategy on an authority-wide basis and through local area youth councils. In Bury, this has led to a young people's strategy, which aims to tackle the problems facing young people, including lack of places to go, lack of things to do and lack of transport, as well as reducing crime and nuisance. A central theme of the strategy is 'citizenship', in school and in the local community. Those who are less likely to participate through official channels are contacted on the streets, through outreach work. Other important themes include providing co-ordinated advice and information to young people and improving the facilities that young people want; and targeting available resources on those who are most at risk, by providing facilities in deprived areas and special projects on housing, training and employment. All local agencies are committed to the strategy and the local authority has agreed funding for the first three years, for which bids can be made.

Funding

166. The Single Regeneration Budget Challenge Fund can be a very useful source of funding for community safety schemes that form part of a comprehensive strategy for local regeneration, with £1.3 billion available from 1996/97 to 1998/99. Co-operation at the local level is a requirement, and the involvement of the police and the probation service is seen to be increasingly important. About half of the successful bids so far have included community safety initiatives.

Conclusions

167. The elements of a comprehensive strategy for preventing youth crime, and considering the development of caution plus action schemes for young people who start to establish a pattern of offending, require action across the board. Each area will have to work out its own priorities, but the establishment of a local forum for planning should at least allow the various agencies to work out a programme together. Not only would this enable them to reduce the time spent on processing offenders, but it could also faciliate a consistent approach to effective work with offenders and those at risk of offending.

168. The Government has established a ministerial group on juveniles, which is focusing on what can be done to stop children drifting into crime, and looking at departmental policies and programmes to identify any gaps or difficulties in delivering an effective service to those at risk (Ref.129). In addition, central government should help by:

- giving local authorities a duty to convene interagency groups;
- requiring other agencies to co-operate with such groups – in particular, to provide information about offending behaviour to help target and evaluate preventive schemes;
- encouraging local services to develop caution plus schemes to address offending by young people; and
- considering how any savings to centrally funded services from the more efficient processing of offenders can be released to fund more effective measures for dealing with offenders and preventing offending in the first place.

169. Achieving any of these objectives is unlikely to be straightforward, as it will require co-ordination between the Department of the Environment, the Department of Health, the Department for Education and Employment, the Home Office, Lord Chancellor's Department, the Crown Prosecution Service and the Welsh Office. How this is achieved is a matter for central government. It could, for example, give a minister and/or official the responsibility for a range of options, such as:

- implementing the recommendations for central government outlined above;
- ensuring that departments pursue common objectives for dealing with crime and antisocial behaviour by young people;
- acting as a contact point for local services dealing with young people which identify differences in approach between different parts of central government that impede their work;
- collecting and publicising evaluations of caution plus programmes; and
- co-ordinating a programme of studies to evaluate interventions intended to reduce offending by young people.

Recommendations

1 Efforts to prevent offending and other antisocial behaviour by young people need to be co-ordinated between the different agencies involved; they should also be targeted on deprived areas with high crime rates, and piloted and evaluated.

2 Local authority chief executives should consider initiating forums in which all relevant local authority services and other agencies participate, to develop a strategy for addressing and preventing youth crime and oversee any multi-agency caution plus schemes.

3 Local chief officers and other policymakers need to determine the scope for collaboration and set objectives for joint activity, in the light of past and present initiatives and local problems.

4 Managers should consider how best to identify residents' needs in the priority areas that have been identified, and practical ways of addressing them, making sure that local residents – including young people – have the opportunity to contribute their views.

5 Practitioners need to see the value of the multi-agency approach and understand the aims of other services dealing with young people. Joint training of practitioners working in the target areas can help promote shared understanding and help identify shared problems.

6 As a minimum, local authorities should ensure that they have strategies, formulated and agreed by all the relevant services, in the context of children's services plans, for encouraging children in their areas not to commit criminal offences.

7 All agencies should ensure that they have taken the necessary steps to share any relevant information with others who are dealing with young offenders.

8 Central government should help by:

- giving local authorities a duty to convene interagency groups;

- giving other agencies a duty to co-operate with such groups – in particular, to provide information about offending behaviour to help target and evaluate preventive schemes;

- encouraging local services to develop caution plus schemes to address offending by young people; and

- considering how any savings from the more efficient processing of offenders can be diverted to fund more effective measures for dealing with offenders and preventing offending in the first place.

9 Co-ordination would be needed between the Department of the Environment, the Department of Health, the Department for Education and Employment, the Home Office, the Lord Chancellor's Department, the Crown Prosecution Service and the Welsh Office.

Appendix 1

Research on what works to reduce re-offending

What works?

The features of effective programmes are:

- approaches based on behavioural or cognitive-behavioural methods;

- approaches which are community-based, to enable proximity to the offender's home environment and real life learning;

- matching of the level of risk posed by the individual (based on offending history and perhaps other characteristics) with the level of the intervention;

- a recognition that specific factors are associated with offending, and that these should be treated separately from other needs;

- using a learning style which requires active participation on the part of the offender, but is also carefully structured;

- skills-oriented, in order to teach problem solving and social interaction, including role play and modelling;

- employment-focused, where offenders can obtain real jobs (based on Lipsey's analysis);

- those which have clear aims and which are linked consistently with the methods used;

- broad, in order to address the range of offenders' problems;

The amount of treatment is important: interventions of six months or more, with at least two contacts with the offender each week and/or more than 100 total contact hours, are significantly more likely to produce good results with high-risk offenders than interventions with less contact (Ref. A2). Gendreau (Ref. A3) recommends that intensive services should occupy 40-70 per cent of a high-risk offender's time over three to nine months; that is around 300 or so hours to complete the programme. Lower risk individuals need less intensive intervention (Ref. A1).

Treatments associated with the criminal justice system are slightly better than those which are completely independent, possibly because they deal with a group which has more scope to improve (Ref. A2). Programmes that address offending behaviour instead of processing through the courts give the best results (Ref. A4). Programmes conducted in the community rather than in institutions tend to have positive effects because it is easier to relate lessons learned on such programmes to real life situations (Ref. A5).

Other features associated with more successful programmes are:

(i)   having **consistent aims and methods.** Keeping to a consistent, standard approach makes programmes easier to evaluate and remain high in 'integrity'. Left to themselves, practitioners are likely to adapt programmes to suit the needs of the offender group. For example, some individuals find the literacy required of them to complete cognitive-behavioural programmes (such as reasoning and rehabilitation) too demanding and are unable to concentrate in a classroom situation (Ref. A5).

(ii)   being carried out by **specially trained practitioners.** Practitioners should be selected on the basis of interpersonal skills such as communication skills, warmth, openness and the ability to set appropriate limits. Their training should cover theories of criminal behaviour, its prediction and treatment; in-service training of several months should include the application of specific and general behavioural interventions (Ref. A3).

(iii)   keeping the **initiators of the programmes involved** throughout their implementation. Studies in which the researchers are more closely involved also lead to better results. This could be due to the enthusiasm generated by a closely researched project, as well as more control of the interventions and closer monitoring (Ref. A2).

Examples of methods that have produced good results include:

(i)   behavioural approaches, such as reward and reinforcement, family contracting, and family teaching programmes to reduce stealing and aggression; also modelling, graduated practice, rehearsal, role play.

(ii)   training in moral reasoning, which has been used to reduce antisocial attitudes, hostility and violence, and leads to more widespread positive changes in young offenders.

(iii)   mixed programmes which use behavioural and cognitive components. A package developed in Canada, called Reasoning and Rehabilitation, has shown considerable reduction in re-offending nine months later (18 per cent as opposed to 70 per cent). It comprises 35 two-hour sessions to teach cognitive skills, social and self-control, negotiation, creative thinking and critical reasoning. The STOP programme in Mid Glamorgan (Ref. A6) is also based on reasoning and rehabilitation (Ref. A7). Probation officers received four to five days training, with training and supervision from consultants where some sessions were videotaped and feedback given. Here, the approach gave less impressive results than the original study but showed better outcomes than had any other interventions, including probation, community service or custody. The programme depends on a reasonable level of literacy in the participants, so some other areas have chosen not to use it in its original form.

(iv)   relapse prevention, an approach which started in the alcoholism field. It involves practising pro-social behaviours in risky situations and rewarding competencies. Significant others, family and friends can be trained to provide reinforcement for appropriate behaviour. Booster sessions can be given at intervals.

(v)   social skills training, which can be a helpful component for many, including those with family conflicts, sex offenders and problem drinkers. Anger control training is important for those with violent behaviour and self-control training can help to reduce stealing and shoplifting.

(vi)   therapeutic approaches, such as relaxation and systematic desensitisation, can help offenders with more 'pathological' patterns of behaviour, such as specifically motivated hostility (for example, racial), and aggression while driving (Ref. A1).

Work with offenders needs to address a broad range of their needs and problems. Even very good cognitive-behavioural work needs to be supported by a variety of problem-solving approaches, supported by community resources (Ref. A8). Those at higher risk of re-offending are usually found to be more influenced by intensive programmes, which may be due to the greater potential for improvement in this group (Ref. A9). Low-risk individuals often do better with less intensive programmes. So targeting high-risk offenders with the most intensive programmes is likely to be cost effective.

What kinds of offender are most influenced? Static factors, such as age and personal history cannot be changed. Dynamic factors which are associated with persistent offending and can be influenced include:

◆ antisocial attitudes and beliefs;
◆ temperamental factors such as impulsivity, egocentrism, weak problem-solving skills and restless, aggressive energy;
◆ low levels of educational and vocational achievement;
◆ peers involved in crime and an absence of non-criminal peers; and
◆ substance abuse.

Potential protective factors include high IQ and doing well in school (Ref. A3).

Effective approaches usually aim for intermediate targets that are related to the dynamic risk factors. They should match the offender's likelihood of re-offending, needs and problems, and individual learning styles. Structured behavioural approaches are best for those who are less interpersonally skilled; verbally expressive methods are better for those with greater skills; and approaches which are not too confrontational are suitable for those who are interpersonally anxious. Promising targets include:

◆ changing antisocial attitudes;
◆ changing antisocial feelings;
◆ reducing antisocial peer associations;
◆ promoting family affection and communication;
◆ promoting family supervision and monitoring;
◆ promoting identification and association with anti-criminal role models;
◆ increasing self-control, self-management and problem-solving skills;

- replacing the skills of lying, stealing and aggression with more pro-social alternatives;
- reducing chemical dependencies;
- rewarding non-criminal activities in family, academic, work and leisure settings;
- ensuring that the client can recognise risky situations and has a plan for dealing with them; and
- providing those who have chronic psychiatric problems with appropriate help.

Intermediate targets that are not directly associated with offending behaviour are less promising. Examples include:

- increasing self-esteem without reducing antisocial thinking and peer associations;
- focusing on emotional and personal problems that are not linked with criminal acts;
- increasing the cohesiveness of antisocial peer groups, as in 'therapeutic' groups;
- improving neighbourhood living conditions, without focusing on criminal behaviour;
- indicating that the values of an antisocial culture may be as valid as those of a pro-social culture;
- increasing conventional ambitions in school and work without concrete assistance in realising them; and
- attempting to turn the client into a 'better person' as defined in ways unconnected with criminality (Ref. A10).

Poor motivation should be considered as an intermediate target for change, rather than a reason not to include an individual in a programme.

Most of the successful programmes have been developed in the USA and Canada, as well as some in Germany and other European countries. Behavioural and cognitive-behavioural approaches – major features of them all – have been developed by psychologists and are based on learning theories. Psychologists also have a tradition of research and evaluation of the effects of interventions, but none is employed in probation or youth justice services in England and Wales. A few are to be found in the prison service; otherwise, they tend to be restricted to the arena of healthcare or to education. The knowledge and expertise of psychologists should be used by social services in this country to devise, implement and monitor behavioural and cognitive-behavioural programmes in community settings.

What does not work?

Approaches that use general counselling, casework, family counselling and psychodynamic therapy based on gaining insight are particularly ineffective. The lack of success of counselling may be explained by the fact that psychological changes are not necessarily matched by reduced re-offending.

Behavioural change appears to be more strongly influenced by behavioural approaches (Ref. A9). Unstructured groups also tend to be ineffective as they may foster communications which reinforce offending behaviour (Ref. A5).

Exclusively punishment-based programmes such as shock incarceration, intense surveillance and home confinement have been found to lead to less successful outcomes (Ref. A9). McGuire (Ref. A1) notes that if punishment is to have a substantial effect on subsequent behaviour it needs to be immediate, comprehensible to the individual and should show the way to alternative ways of behaving.

Imprisonment can, in principle, reduce offending by deterring others and by keeping prolific offenders out of circulation. Specific evidence regarding the deterrence argument is hard to identify, however, given the complexity of motives for crime. And comparisons of different states in the USA and comparisons of the same state under different policy regimes have shown no link between the rates of imprisonment and crime (Ref. A11). The incapacitation argument depends on the rate at which individuals would have committed crimes if given an alternative disposal, the time period for which they are locked up, and the effects on their recidivism when they are released.

The main study from the UK (Ref. A12) has compared the effectiveness in reducing re-offending of 'Intermediate Treatment (IT)' – either as an alternative to custody (heavy-end IT) or otherwise – with that of custody (after release) or straight supervision orders, for equivalent groups of offenders. IT that was organised by a single centre appeared slightly better than custody, but the results were not statistically significant. This may reflect:

- a comparatively small sample size;
- the absence of a clear focus on reducing offending – most programmes evaluated gave 'providing an alternative to custody' as their main aim and a few, 'changing attitudes';
- the least effective programme was not run from a dedicated centre, but consisted of a package of treatment elements provided by different units or individuals, including a befriending scheme, individual counselling, a motor project, reparation and individual work on offending behaviour. Its lack of success is consistent with Whitehead and Lab's observation that programmes which relied on referral to other, 'non-system', agencies were the least effective in reducing re-offending (Ref. A4). It would also have been less able to provide a consistent message, based on the authority of individual staff members and 'pro-social modelling';
- the intensity of programmes varied but not consistently, in line with the degree of criminality of the offenders. Matching programmes more carefully to offenders may have produced better results; and/or
- offenders' personal and social problems, as measured on a checklist, were significantly worse in the custody group, one year after treatment, than in any of the community-based programmes.

The overall costs of the various treatments were very similar. Custody was slightly more expensive than either ordinary or heavy-end IT, but the difference was not statistically significant. The weekly costs of IT were considerably lower than those of custody, but the greater length of time involved in the community treatments brought the total costs to about level. Since the amount of treatment seems to be an important feature of effective programmes, community interventions are not, in fact, a cheap alternative to custody.

References

A1.   J McGuire, *What Works: Reducing Re-offending*, Wiley, Chichester, 1995.

A2.   M Lipsey, 'What Do We Learn From 400 Research Studies on the Effectiveness of Treatment with Juvenile Delinquents?', in J McGuire, *What Works: Reducing Re-offending*, Wiley, Chichester, 1995.

A3.   P Gendreau, 'What Works in Community Corrections: Promising Approaches in Reducing Criminal Behaviour', *IARCA Journal*, vol 6, 1995, pp 5-12.

A4.   J Whitehead and S Lab, 'A Meta-analysis of Juvenile Correction Treatment', *Journal of Research in Crime and Delinquency*, vol 26, 3, 1989, pp 276-295.

A5.   D Andrews, I Zinger, R Hoge, J Bonta, P Gendreau, F Cullen, 'Does Correctional Treatment Work? A Clinically Relevant and Psychologically Informed Meta-analysis', *Criminology*, vol 28, 3, 1990, pp 369-404.

A6.   C Knott, 'The STOP Programme: Reasoning and Rehabilitation in a British Setting', in J McGuire, *What Works: Reducing Re-offending*, Wiley, Chichester, 1995.

A7.   R Ross, E Fabiano and C Ewles, 'Reasoning and Rehabilitation', *International Journal of Offender Therapy and Comparative Criminology*, 1988, pp 29 – 35.

A8.   D Sutton, *The Essential Ingredients of Offender Programmes*, Cognitive Centre Foundation, South Glamorgan, 1995.

A9.   M Lipsey, Juvenile Delinquency Treatment: 'A Meta-analytic Inquiry Into The Variability of Effects', In T Cook et al (eds), *Meta-analysis for Explanation: A Casebook*, New York, Russell Sage Foundation, 1992.

A10.   D Andrews, 'The Psychology of Criminal Conduct and Effective Treatment', in McGuire, *What Works: Reducing Re-offending*, Wiley, Chichester, 1995.

A11.   Zimring, cited in 'Crime in America', *The Economist*, 8 June 1996.

A12.   A Bottoms, *Intensive Community Supervision for Young Offenders: Outcomes, Process and Costs,* University of Cambridge, Institute of Criminology, 1995.

Appendix 2

Members of the Advisory Panel

- Barry Anderson, NACRO
- Tony Christopher, ex-Audit Commissioner
- Charles Clark, Assistant Chief Constable, Essex Police
- Felicity Clarkson, Juvenile Offenders Unit, Home Office
- Frances Crook, Howard League
- Anthony Douglas, London Borough of Havering Social Services
- Henry Giller, Social Information Systems
- John Graham, Research and Planning Unit, Home Office
- Jean Grainger, Youth and Community Services, Buckinghamshire
- Ann Hagell, Policy Studies Institute
- John Harding, Inner London Probation Service
- Nick Lacey, National Audit Office
- Chris Sealey, Social Services Inspectorate, Department of Health
- Helena Shovelton, Audit Commissioner

References

1. C Mirrlees-Black, P Mayhew and A Percy, *The 1996 British Crime Survey: England and Wales*, Home Office, 1996.

2. P Mayhew, N Aye Maung and C Mirrlees Black, *The 1992 British Crime Survey,* Home Office Research Study No.132, 1993.

3. P Mayhew, C Mirrlees-Black and N Aye Maung, *Trends in Crime: Findings from the 1994 British Crime Survey*, Research Findings No. 14, Home Office, 1994.

4. C Mirrlees-Black, P Mayhew and A Percy, *The 1996 British Crime Survey: England and Wales*, Home Office Statistical Bulletin 19/96, Home Office, 1996.

5. C Mirlees-Black and A Ross, *Crime Against Retail Premises in 1993*, Home Office Research Findings No. 26, Home Office, 1995.

6. C Mirlees-Black and A Ross, *Crime Against Manufacturing Premises in 1993*, Home Office Research Findings No. 27, Home Office, 1995.

7. Coopers and Lybrand, *Preventative Strategy for Young People in Trouble*, The Prince's Trust, 1994.

8. Home Office, *Digest 3: Information on the Criminal Justice System in England and Wales*, Home Office, 1995.

9. J Graham and B Bowling, *Young People and Crime*, Home Office Research and Planning Unit, Home Office, 1995.

10. A Hagell and T Newburn, *Persistent Young Offenders*, Policy Studies Institute, 1994.

11. M Little, *Young Offenders: Different Groups and Different Interventions*, Dartington Social Research Unit, 1995.

12. *Hansard*, 5/2/96.

13. N Aye Maung, *Young People, Victimisation, and the Police: Summary Findings,* Home Office Research Findings No. 17, Home Office, 1995.

14. G Boswell, *Violent Victims*, The Prince's Trust, 1995.

15. G Farrell and K Pease, *Once Bitten, Twice Bitten: Repeat Victimisation and its Implications for Crime Prevention*, Crime Prevention Paper No. 46, Home Office, 1993.

16. M Hough, 'The Impact of Victimisation: Findings from the British Crime Survey', *Victimology*, Vol. 10, 1985.

17. T Hope, 'Communities, Crime and Inequality in England and Wales', in T Bennett (ed), *Preventing Crime and Disorder*, Institute of

Criminology, Cambridge Cropwood Series, University of Cambridge, 1996.

18. Home Affairs Committee, *Juvenile Offenders*, Sixth Report, HMSO, 1993.

19. Home Office, *Criminal Statistics: England and Wales 1994*, Home Office, 1995.

20. Projections supplied by Government Actuary's Department.

21. Audit Commission, *Streetwise*, Audit Commission, London, 1996.

22. Home Office, *Protecting the Public*, Cm 3190, Home Office, 1996.

23. ACC, AMA, ADSS, NACRO, ACOP, *National Protocol for Youth Justice Services*, AMA, London, 1996.

24. D Brown, T Ellis and K Larcombe, *Changing the Code: Police Detention under the Revised PACE Codes of Practice*, Home Office Research Study 129, Home Office, London, 1992.

25. Legal Aid Board, correspondence with National Audit Office, June 1996.

26. ACPO Crime Committee, *The Cautioning of Offenders*, ACPO, London, 1995.

27. Home Office, *The Criminal Histories of Those Cautioned in 1985, 1988 and 1991*, Home Office, 1994.

28. Home Office, *The Cautioning of Offenders*, Circular 18/94, Home Office, 1994.

29. Audit Commission, *Helping with Enquiries*, Audit Commission, London, 1993.

30. Crown Prosecution Service, review by Price Waterhouse of new joint performance management arrangements (CPS correspondence) July 1996.

31. Social Services Inspectorate (personal correspondence) 1996.

32. Department of Health, *Guidance on Permissible Forms of Control in Children's Residential Care*, LAC (93)13, 1993.

33. Crown Prosecution Service, review of discontinuance in the Birmingham branch (CPS correspondence) July 1996.

34. D Crisp and D Moxon, *Case Screening by the Crown Prosecution Service: How and Why Cases are Terminated*, Home Office Research Study No. 137, Home Office, 1994.

35. J Shapland, J Hibbert, J l'Anson, A Sorsby and R Wild, *Milton Keynes Criminal Justice Audit*, Institute for the Study of the Legal Profession, University of Sheffield, 1995.

36. Home Office, *Probation Statistics: England and Wales*, Home Office, 1993.

37. C Stanley, *National Survey of Youth Justice Arrangements*, NACRO, London, 1996.

38. NACRO, *Bail Support Directory*, NACRO, London, 1995.

39. Howard League, *Banged Up, Beaten Up, Cutting Up,* Report of the Howard League Commission of Inquiry into the Evidence in Penal Institutions for Young People, Howard League, London, 1995.

40. Board of Visitors of Feltham Young Offenders Institution, *Annual Report for 1995*, 1996.

41. Lord Chancellor's Department, *Defendants in the Youth Court*, correspondence, 30 September 1996.

42. Home Office, *Criminal Statistics: England and Wales*, HMSO, 1994.

43. Lord Chancellor's Department, *Striking the Balance: The Future of Legal Aid in England and Wales*, Cm 3305, HMSO, 1996.

44. B Eames, A Hooke and D Portas, *Court Attendance by Police Officers*, Police Research Series, Home Office Police Department, Home Office, 1995.

45. Home Office, Department of Health and Welsh Office, *National Standards for the Supervision of Offenders in the Community*, Home Office, 1995.

46. J McGuire, *What Works: Reducing Re-offending*, Wiley, Chichester, 1995.

47. M Lipsey, 'Juvenile Delinquency Treatment: A Meta-analytic Inquiry into the Variability of Effects', in T Cook et al (eds), *Meta-analysis for Explanation: A Casebook*, New York, Russell Sage Foundation, 1992.

48. D Andrews, I Zinger, R Hoge, J Bonta, P Gendreau, F Cullen, 'Does Correctional Treatment Work? A Clinically Relevant and Psychologically Informed Meta-analysis', *Criminology*, Vol. 28, 3, pp369-404, 1990.

49. Home Office, *Criminal Statistics Supplementary Tables: Volume 1,* Table S1.7(A), Government Statistical Service, HMSO, 1993.

50. Justices' Clerks' Society and Magistrates' Association, *Guidance on Binding Over the Parents of Young People Prosecuted in the Youth Court*, Magistrates' Association, London, 30 September 1996.

51. Home Office, *Prison Statistics in England and Wales*, Cm 2893, HMSO, 1993.

52. B Stewart and L Gaynor, *Indicators of Youth Crime in Gloucestershire*, Gloucestershire Social Services, 1996.

53. Home Office, *Costs of the Criminal Justice System*, Home Office, 1992.

54. M Fitzgerald, *Ethnic Minorities and the Criminal Justice System*, Royal Commission on Criminal Justice, HMSO, 1993.

55.   H McCulloch, *An Evaluation of the Retail Theft Initiative at Milton Keynes*, Home Office, 1996.

56.   E Currie, *Is America Really Winning the War on Crime and Should Britain Follow its Example?*, 30th anniversary lecture, NACRO, London, 1996.

57.   A Morris and G Maxwell, 'Juvenile Justice in New Zealand: A New Paradigm', *Australian and New Zealand Journal of Criminology*, 26, 1993, pp72-90.

58.   F. Robinson, 'Persistent Young Offenders', *Youth and Policy*, Vol. 48, pp84-8, 1995.

59.   D Farrington, *Understanding and Preventing Youth Crime*, Joseph Rowntree Foundation, York, 1996.

60.   Farrington et al, 1990, cited in H Yoshikawa, 'Prevention as Cumulative Protection: Effects of Early Family Support and Education on Chronic Delinquency and Its Risks', *Psychological Bulletin*, Vol. 115, 1994, pp28-54.

61.   Rutter et al, 1979, also Kolvin et al, 1990, cited in H Yoshikawa, 'Prevention as Cumulative Protection: Effects of Early Family Support and Education on Chronic Delinquency and its Risks', *Psychological Bulletin*, Vol. 115, 1994, pp28-54.

62.   OECD, *Income Distribution in OECD Countries*, OECD, Paris, 1995.

63.   J Walsh, *What Price A Child*, ASDA, 1996.

64.   G Pugh, E De'Ath and C Smith, *Confident Parents, Confident Children*, National Children's Bureau, London, 1994.

65.   A Hirschfield, *Crime and Disadvantage in North West England*, Presentation to National Institute of Justice, Washington DC, 8 November 1995.

66.   Wadsworth, 1979, cited in D Utting, J Bright and C Henricson, *Crime and the Family*, Family Policy Studies Centre, London, 1979.

67.   Kolvin et al, 1990, cited in D Utting, J Bright and C Henricson, *Crime and the Family*, Family Policy Studies Centre, London, 1993.

68.   Booth et al, 1992, cited in H Yoshikawa, 'Prevention as Cumulative Protection: Effects of Early Family Support and Education on Chronic Delinquency and Its Risks', *Psychological Bulletin*, Vol. 115, 1994, pp28-54.

69.   Rutter et al, 1979, cited in H Yoshikawa, 'Prevention as Cumulative Protection: Effects of Early Family Support and Education on Chronic Delinquency and Its Risks', *Psychological Bulletin*, Vol. 115, 1994, pp28-54.

70. Lewis et al, 1989, cited in H Yoshikawa, 'Prevention as Cumulative Protection: Effects of Early Family Support and Education on Chronic Delinquency and Its Risks', *Psychological Bulletin*, Vol. 115, 1994, pp28-54.

71. West and Farrington, 1973, cited in D Farrington, 'Early Developmental Prevention of Juvenile Delinquency', *Criminal Behaviour and Mental Health*, Vol. 4, 1994, pp209-27.

72. Farrington, 1978, cited in D Farrington, 'Human Development and Criminal Careers', in M Maguire, R Morgan and R Reiner (eds), *The Oxford Handbook of Criminology*, Clarendon Press, Oxford, 1994.

73. Craig and Glick, 1968, cited in D Farrington, 'Human Development and Criminal Careers', in M Maguire, R Morgan and R Reiner (eds), *The Oxford Handbook of Criminology*, Clarendon Press, Oxford, 1994.

74. Kolvin et al, 1990, cited in D Farrington, 'Human Development and Criminal Careers', in M Maguire, R Morgan and R Reiner (eds), *The Oxford Handbook of Criminology*, Clarendon Press, Oxford, 1994.

75. McCord, 1982, cited in D Farrington, 'Human Development and Criminal Careers', in M Maguire, R Morgan and R Reiner (eds), *The Oxford Handbook of Criminology*, Clarendon Press, Oxford, 1994.

76. Wadsworth, 1979, cited in D Farrington, 'Human Development and Criminal Careers', in M Maguire, R Morgan and R Reiner (eds), *The Oxford Handbook of Criminology*, Clarendon Press, Oxford, 1994.

77. D Butterworth, 'Are fathers really necessary to the family unit in early childhood?', *Journal of Early Childhood*, Vol. 26, 1, 1994, pp1-5.

78. Honig, 1977, cited in J McGuire and F Earls, 'Prevention of Psychiatric Disorder in Early Childhood', *Journal of Child Psychology and Psychiatry*, Vol. 32, 1, 1991, pp129-54.

79. Alexander and Parsons, 1973, cited in D Farrington, 'Early Developmental Prevention of Juvenile Delinquency', *Criminal Behaviour and Mental Health*, Vol. 4, 1994, pp209-27.

80. Provence and Naylor, 1983, cited in J McGuire and F Earls, 'Prevention of Psychiatric Disorder in Early Childhood', *Journal of Child Psychology and Psychiatry*, Vol. 32, 1,1992, pp129-54.

81. W van der Eyken, *Homestart, a Four-Year Evaluation*, Homestart, Leicester, 1982.

82. Audit Commission, *Seen But Not Heard*, Audit Commission, London, 1994.

83. Department of Health and Welsh Office, *Children Act Report*, 1994, HMSO, Cm 2878, 1995.

84. C Green, *Toddler Taming*, Vermilion, 1992.

85. R Skinner and J Cleese, *Families and How to Survive Them*, Methuen, 1993.

86. McGee et al, 1984, cited in D Farrington, 'Early Developmental Prevention of Juvenile Delinquency', *Criminal Behaviour and Mental Health*, Vol. 4, 1994, pp209-27.

87. Stattin and Klackenberg-Larsson, 1993, cited in D Farrington, 'Early Developmental Prevention of Juvenile Delinquency', *Criminal Behaviour and Mental Health*, Vol. 4, 1994, pp209-27.

88. Farrington, Loeber and Van Kammen, 1990, cited in D Farrington, 'Human Development and Criminal Careers', in M Maguire, R Morgan and R Reiner (eds), *The Oxford Handbook of Criminology*, Clarendon Press, Oxford, 1994.

89. A Kasdin, T Siegel and D Bass, 'Cognitive Problem-Solving Skills Training and Parent Management Training in the Treatment of Antisocial Behaviour in Children', *Journal of Consulting and Clinical Psychology*, Vol. 60, 5, 1992, pp733-47.

90. Z Kurtz, R Thornes and S Wolkind, *Services for the Mental Health of Children and Young People in England: a National Review*, Dept of Public Health, South Thames RHA, London, 1994.

91. Berrueta-Clement et al, 1987, cited in J McGuire and F Earls, 'Prevention of Psychiatric Disorder in Early Childhood', *Journal of Child Psychology and Psychiatry*, Vol. 32, 1, 1991, pp129-54.

92. Farrington, 1982, cited in D Farrington, 'Human Development and Criminal Careers', in M Maguire, R Morgan and R Reiner (eds), *The Oxford Handbook of Criminology*, Clarendon Press, Oxford, 1994.

93. B Stewart, *Links Between Exclusion and Offending in One County – Preliminary Findings* (personal communication), 1996.

94. I Brodie, *Exclusion from School*, Highlight, NCB and Barnardos, London, 1995.

95. C Parsons, *School Exclusion Rates and Measures of Disadvantage*, (personal communication), 1996.

96. D Gillborn, *Racism and Exclusions from School*, Institute of Education, University of London, 1995.

97. D O'Keefe, *Truancy in English Secondary Schools*, University of North London Truancy Unit, London, 1993.

98. DfEE, *National Pupil Absence Tables*, 1995.

99. E Lewis, *Truancy, the Partnership Approach*, Staffordshire Police, 1995.

100. M Rutter et al, *Fifteen Thousand Hours: Secondary Schools and their Effects on Children*, Open Books, 1979.

101.	Kellam et al, 1991, cited in D Offord and J Bennett , 'Conduct Disorder: Long Term Outcomes And Intervention Effectiveness', *Journal of the American Academy of Child and Adolescent Psychiatry*, Vol. 33, 8, 1994, pp1069-79.

102.	Health Advisory Service, *Together We Stand*, HMSO, 1995.

103.	National Association of Social Workers in Education , *NASWE Data Book*, NASWE, 1996.

104.	J Learmonth, *More Willingly to School?*, DfEE, London, 1995.

105.	I Brodie and D Berridge, *School Exclusion: a Report of a Research Seminar*, University of Luton, 1996.

106.	C Parsons, *Final Report to the DfEE on National Survey of LEAs' Policies and Procedures for Children Who are Out of School*, 1995.

107.	M Banks et al, *Careers and Identities*, Open University Press, Milton Keynes, 1992.

108.	D Riley and M Shaw, 1985, cited in D Utting, J Bright and C Henricson, *Crime and the Family*, Family Policy Studies Centre, London, 1993.

109.	Education Act, 1944, sections 41 and 53.

110.	Sufficiency Working Group, *Planning for a Sufficient Youth Service*, Sufficiency Working Group, Coventry, 1994.

111.	J Barrett and R Greenway, *Why Adventure?*, Foundation for Outdoor Adventure, Coventry, 1995.

112.	Ofsted, *Youth Work Responses to Young People at Risk*, Ofsted, London, 1993.

113.	Centrepoint, *New Picture of Youth Homelessness*, Centrepoint, London, 1996.

114.	J Smith and S Gilford, *Homelessness Among under-25s*, Joseph Rowntree Foundation, York, 1991.

115.	Trust for the Study of Adolescence, *Young People at Risk, an Agenda for Action*, Trust for the Study of Adolescence, Brighton, 1994.

116.	N Biehal, J Clayton, M Stein, J Wade, *Prepared for Living?*, Leaving Care Research Project, Leeds University, 1992.

117.	L Garnett, *Leaving Care and After*, National Children's Bureau, London, 1992.

118.	A West, *You're on Your Own, Young People's Research on Leaving Care*, Save the Children, London, 1995.

119.	First Key, *A Survey of Local Authority Provisions for Young People Leaving Care*, First Key, Leeds, 1992.

120.   N Biehal, J Clayton, M Stein, J Wade, *Moving On*, HMSO, 1995.

121.   South Glamorgan TEC, *Young People not in Education, Training or Employment in South Glamorgan*, S.Glamorgan TEC, 1994.

122.   Coalition on Young People and Social Security, *Six Years of Hardship, an Update*, Children's Society, London, 1995.

123.   Annabel Jackson Associates, *Foyers, the Step in the Right Direction*, Foyer Federation for Youth, London, 1996.

124.   D Levine, *I've Started So I'll Finish*, Community Self Build Agency, London, 1994.

125.   M Ramsay and A Percy, *Drug Misuse Declared: Results of the 1994 British Crime Survey*, Home Office Research Study No. 151, Home Office, 1996.

126.   R Matthews and J Trickey, *Drugs and Crime: a Study Amongst Young People in Leicester*, University of Leicester, Centre for the Study of Public Order, 1996.

127.   F Fukuyama, *Trust: the Social Virtues and the Creation of Prosperity*, Hamish Hamilton, London, 1995.

128.   ACC, ADC, AMA, and LGMB, *Survey of Community Safety Activities in Local Government in England and Wales*, LGMB, Luton, 1996.

129.   Home Office, *Annual Report 1996*, HMSO, 1996.

Index

References are to paragraph numbers and Boxes.

Absolute discharge   55

Abuse. *See* Child abuse

Adjournments   43-4

Advance disclosure   40

African Caribbeans   71-2, 100

Age of criminal responsibility   29

Aggressive behaviour   76, 96

Alcohol   143-7

American experience   *Box G*, 75

Antisocial behaviour   17, 79, 151, 153, 157, *Box R*

Area Criminal Justice Liaison Committees (ACJLCs)   156

Arrest and interview   25-6

Association of Chief Police Officers (ACPO)   30, 38

Attendance centre orders   61, 68

Bail   36, 45-8

Bail support service   45

Behavioural problems   86, 94, 102, 111, 112

Binding over   59-60

Bottom-up co-ordination   164

British Crime Survey 1992   10

British Crime Survey 1996   1

Bullying in schools   105, 122

BUMPY Project, Kirklees   *Box D*, 65

Burglary   10

Care leavers   129-33

Cases withdrawn, discontinued or dismissed   37-8, 55

'Caution plus' schemes   33, 73, 74, 154, 157

Cautioning   31-3, 38, 73

Central government   168-9

Centrepoint   129

Child abuse   9, 86, 128

Child and adolescent mental health services (CAMHS)   94, 95, 106

Child protection   91

Childhood behaviour   79, 93-6

Children, future criminal trends   12, 15, 79

Children Act 1989   22, 91, 130, 155

Children and Young Persons Act 1933   22

Children and Young Persons Act 1993   8

Children in need   22

Children's Hearings System   *Box H*

Cities in Schools   *Box K*, 115

City Challenge   63

Combination orders   66

Community groups   72

Community institutions   148-9

Community safety   *Box R*, 19, 159, 164, 165

Community sentences   66

Community service orders   66

Compensation   59-60, 74, *Box E, Box F*

Conditional discharge   55

Conduct disorders   95

Constructive activities   120

Co-ordinating programmes   155-9, 169

Costs involved in dealing with young offenders   70

Counselling   57, 111

Crime prevention. *See* Prevention of youth crime

Crime rates   11

Crimes against individuals   2

Criminal Justice Act 1988   14

Criminal Justice Act 1991   5, 59, 60, 66, 72

Criminal justice system   14, 16, 17, 22, 23, 40, 151

  and race   71-2

Criminal Procedure and Investigations Act 1996   47

Crown Court   5, 47

Crown Prosecution Service (CPS)   5, 28, 35, 37, 38, 51, 55

Custodial sentences   67

Custody   74

Dalston Youth Project, Hackney *Box C*, 65

Dance in Action   *Box M*, 126

Data Protection Act 1984   161

Decision-making   27

Delinquency   85, 97

Demographic change   14

Deprived areas   84, 92, 96, 106, 115, 121, 122, 124, 153, 154, 162, 165

  see also High-risk areas

Discipline   86, 96

Disruptive behaviour   96, 106

Diversion Unit. *See* Northamptonshire Diversion Unit

DoE Index of Local Conditions   84

Drop-in facility   123

Drug Action Teams   146, 147

Drugs   *Box P*, 143-7

Education Act 1933   108

Education provision   46, 118

Educational problems   118

Educational psychology/psychologists

Education welfare officers   108

Employment   134-42

Ethnic monitoring information   72

Evaluations   81, 109, 154

Exam passes   102

Family attachment   88

Family centres   90-2

Family conflict   86, 87

Family disputes   128

Family factors   83-92

Family Group Conferences   *Box I*, 75

Family influences   119

Family members, engaging in crime   87, 119

Family relationships 86, 88, 133

Family support 89-91, 96, 110

Fines 59-60, 108

First offenders 18, 32, 73

Foster parents 6

Foyer schemes *Box N*, 141

France *Box Q*, 162

Friends, influences of 119

Funding 166

Further education 116, 136, *Box L*

Gini coefficient 83

Good Behaviour Game 105

Grants for Education Support and Training (GEST) programmes 110, *Box K*

Gravity factors 27

HALT scheme *Box F*, 73

Health Advisory Service 95, 106

Health commissioning authorities 95, 106

High-risk areas 11, 84, 96, 106, 151, 157, 160

see also Deprived areas

High Scope project, Michigan, USA 96

Home support 96

Homeless young people 123, 128, 129

Homestart 90, 92

Housing 127-33

Income inequality 83

Individuals, crime against 2

Information sharing 160-1

Intensive programmes 58, 62

InterDependency Group (IDG) 163

Jarman Index of deprivation 95

Joint initiatives 117

Justices Clerks' Society 60

Juvenile nuisance 17, 157, 160

Lawyers 25

Legal action 108

Legal advice 26

Legal aid 5, 26, 43, 49

Leisure activities 120, 125, 126

Leisure time 119

Letter of apology 31

Local audits 78

Local authorities 74, 129, 131, 133, 159, 168

Local authority accommodation 36-7, 46, 47

Local authority chief executives 157

Local authority residential homes 118

Local authority secure units 48, 70

Local education authorities (LEAs) 28, 96, 106, 108, 110, 112-16

Local forum 158

Local residents 158

Local support networks 90

Lone-parent families 83, 87, 89

'Looked after' children 118

Magistrates 53

Magistrates' Association 60

Manslaughter 8

Mental health professionals 95, 106

Mentoring schemes 65, 120

Milton Keynes retail theft initiative 73

Monitoring 68, 72, 108

Motor projects 65

Motorbike offenders *Box D*, 65

Morality. *See* Right and wrong

Move-on accommodation 132

Murder 8

NCH Action for Children Project *Box B*, 132

Newpin 90, 92

Northamptonshire Diversion Unit *Box E*, 73, 74, 157

Nursery education 96

NVQs 137

Offences, reported and recorded 16

Offending behaviour 20-2, 32, 33, 52, 63, 74, 79, 119

Outdoor adventure activities 122

Oxford Family Nurturing Project 90

Paperwork 34, 35

Parent education 89

Parent training programmes 94

Parental conflict 85, 87

Parental responsibilities 19, 108-9

Parental supervision 83, 86, 88

Parental support 96

Parenting

guidance 92

improving 88-92

inadequacy 86

skills 89

Parents of offenders, binding over 60

Persistent offenders 7, 18, 58, 64, 68, 74, 79, 147

Personal crime 11

Pilot schemes 82, 92, 106, 133, 150

Pleas 49

Police action 5, 20, 25, 27, 29, 160

Police bail 36

Police expertise 28

Police records 32

Practical solutions 162-6

Pre-court procedures 24-6

Predicting future behaviour 85

Pre-school education 96

Pre-sentence reports (PSRs) 43, 51-3, 68

Pre-trial reviews 50

Prevention of youth crime 5, 21, 79, 155-9

programmes 81

targeting measures for 80

Prison service 5, 46

Probation 5, 20, 63

Probation officers 62, 66

Probation orders 66

Index

Probation service — 41-2, 52, 53, 64

Property-related offences — 8, 11

Prosecution — 32, 34-8

    see also Youth court process

Psychiatrists — 95

Psychologists — 58

Psychology services — 106

Public agencies — 151

Public disorder — 11

Public services — 4, 19, 28, 79

Punishment — 5, 44, 56, 86

Pupil referral unit — 114

Race — 71-2, 100, 128

Re-arresting — 36

Remand — 45-8

Remedial schooling — 96

Re-offending — 32, 45, 52, 56-68, 73, 74, Appendix 1

Resources, need for shift in — 153-4

Right and wrong — 148-9

Risk factors — 79, 120, 162

    see also High-risk areas

Royal Philanthropic Society — 45

School exclusions — 98-101, 107-17

School interventions — 105

School performance — 97

School problems — 97-118

School support — 104-6

Scottish Children's Hearings System — Box H, 75

Self-build schemes for young people — Box O, 142

Self-esteem — 122

Sentences of the court — 55

Sentencing, efficiency and effectiveness — 68-70

Serious offences — 8, 9

Severe hardship payments — 138

Shoplifting — 73

Single Regeneration Budget Challenge Fund — 166

Social deprivation — 100, 111

Social security benefits — 139

Social services — 6, 20, 22, 25, 28, 36, 91, 92, 110, 117, 118, 133

Social workers — 25, 133

South East Kent Bail Support Scheme — Box A, 45

Special education needs — 99, 112

Special needs unit — 111

Sport — 120

Sports facilities — 125

Statements of special educational need — 106

Step-families — 87

Step-parents — 128

Strategic co-ordination — 163

Strategy development — 152-69

Summer activity schemes — 122, 124

Summons — 37

Supervision orders — 62-5, 68, 88

Support services — 151

Support teachers — 111

Teachers — 104, 106

Theft — 6, 73

Training — 134-42

Training and Enterprise Councils (TECs) — 137

Trials — 50-1

Trials Issues Group — 35

Truancy — 99, 101-3, 107-17

Truancy and Disaffected Pupils programme — 109

Two-parent families — 83

Victim risk — 9-12

Victims — 74, Box E, Box F, Box I

Violence — 9

Voluntary sector — 117, 126, 132, 139

Voluntary organisations — 90

Wandsworth Bail Support service — 45

Warnings — 30

Welfare — 22

Weston Spirit project — Box L, 126

Young adult males — 15

Young offenders — 7-8

    costs involved — 70

    experience and views of — 76-7

    identifying and dealing with — 5, 20-2

    more efficient and effective approach — 73-7

    summary vignettes — Box J, 77

Young people

    at risk — 18, 79

    leaving care — 129-33

Youth clubs — 121

Youth court process — 5, 6, 39-54

    speeding up — 54

Youth crime — 1-6

    prevention. See Prevention of youth crime

    trends — 13-15

Youth justice services — 5, 22, 25, 27, 41-2, 53, 63, 65, 68

Youth services — 120-6

Youth workers — 120-6